CITYSPOTS
BUCH

Thomas Cook

Biserica
Bacur
Cioberul

WHAT'S IN YOUR GUIDEBOOK?

Independent authors Impartial up-to-date information from our travel experts who meticulously source local knowledge.

Experience Thomas Cook's 165 years in the travel industry and guidebook publishing enriches every word with expertise you can trust.

Travel know-how Contributions by thousands of staff around the globe, each one living and breathing travel.

Editors Travel-publishing professionals, pulling everything together to craft a perfect blend of words, pictures, maps and design.

You, the traveller We deliver a practical, no-nonsense approach to information, geared to how you really use it.

● *Bulevardul Unirii, leading up to the huge Casa Popolurui*

CITYSPOTS
BUCHAREST

Craig Turp

Thomas Cook

Written by Craig Turp
Original photography by Craig Turp
Front cover photography (Broken Man statue) © Richard I'Anson/Lonely Planet
Series design based on an original concept by Studio 183 Limited

Produced by Cambridge Publishing Management Limited
Project Editor: Amanda Learmonth
Layout: Paul Queripel
Maps: PC Graphics
Transport map: © Communicarta Limited

Published by Thomas Cook Publishing
A division of Thomas Cook Tour Operations Limited
Company Registration No. 1450464 England
PO Box 227, Unit 18, Coningsby Road
Peterborough PE3 8SB, United Kingdom
email: books@thomascook.com
www.thomascookpublishing.com
+ 44 (0) 1733 416477
ISBN: 978-1-84157-766-1

First edition © 2007 Thomas Cook Publishing
Text © 2007 Thomas Cook Publishing
Maps © 2007 Thomas Cook Publishing
Series/Project Editor: Kelly Anne Pipes
Production/DTP: Steven Collins

Printed and bound in Spain by GraphyCems

CONTENTS

SYMBOLS KEY

The following symbols are used throughout this book:

@ address   ✆ telephone   ⓦ website address   ⓔ email
⏲ opening times   ❶ important

The following symbols are used on the maps:

✈ airport   O city
✚ hospital   O large town
⛊ police station   ○ small town
🚌 bus station   ═ motorway
🚆 railway station   ─ main road
Ⓜ metro   ─ minor road
                       ─ railway

❶ numbers denote featured cafés & restaurants

Hotels and restaurants are graded by approximate price
as follows:
£ budget   ££ mid-range   £££ expensive

❶ Piața Unirii's fountain puts on an attractive display

INTRODUCING
Bucharest

Introduction

Hot and dusty, Bucharest in high summer is more North Africa than Europe; freezing and usually covered with snow for months at a time, in midwinter it's more like the Arctic. Chaos reigns all year round – regardless of the weather – and the dynamism of a city playing catch-up with the rest of the continent can often make the place bewildering; therein lies the charm.

Even its fiercest advocate would readily admit that when taken at face value Bucharest is Europe's most unappealing capital. Very little of the old Bucharest – dubbed Little Paris in the 1920s and 1930s by the procession of famous travellers who came here – remains: the vast majority of the city's buildings date from the communist period, when the need to build hundreds of thousands of apartments at great speed meant aesthetics lost out. Within the socialist realism, however, gems remain: the art deco blocks of Bulevardul Magheru, the neoclassical University and the crumbling secessionist houses of Lipscani, the one part of the Old Town that survived central planning.

But let's be honest, you probably aren't coming for the sights. Instead, most people visit Bucharest for its energy. The place simply buzzes with young and dynamic people from all over Romania; the country's brightest and best all come here to study, and most decide to stay for good on graduation. You'll see evidence of Bucharest's dynamism everywhere, from the construction boom that has seen shiny new skyscrapers appear from nowhere to the trendy nightspots that are attracting the finest DJs in the world.

As life-affirming destinations go, Bucharest is as good as it gets right now, and a weekend is enough to see the few real sights there are. If you do have more time, the palaces that surround the capital make tranquil kickback destinations, while just an hour or so on Romania's new fast trains, the ski slopes of Sinaia await anyone with any energy left in reserve. And we hardly have time to mention that it all comes at bargain prices.

◆ *The shiny Financial Plaza overlooking the Dâmbovița River*

When to go

SEASONS & CLIMATE

Quite simply, when it comes to the weather, Bucharest is a city of extremes. Winters are bitterly cold, with thermometers rarely climbing out of the blue zone from the end of November until the end of March. Snow covers the ground for months on end, and if you are looking for a guaranteed white Christmas then December is a great time to visit. The city never looks better than immediately after a snowfall, when its rougher edges get a charming, frosty frame.

If it exists at all, spring is short in Bucharest. April is either an extension of winter, with temperatures to match, or heralds an early summer, and the city's terraces fill up accordingly. Expect blisteringly hot weather from May to September, well over 30°C (86°F) most of the time. Avoid the place in August at all costs, unless a desire to swelter in 40°C (104°F) heat is on your agenda. The city is all but deserted in August anyway; the good folk of Bucharest head for the mountains or the beach en bloc.

By September's end the pendulum swings backs towards winter, and though autumn gets more of a look-in than spring, do not be surprised to still be drinking spritzers outside in late October, or throwing snowballs early in November.

ANNUAL EVENTS
Spring

On 1 March, Romanians mark the coming of spring by handing a **Mărţişor** (a brooch with a red and white thread attached to it) to every woman or girl they know. Visitors are not excused, so buy plenty of *Mărțișor* well in advance; stalls selling them are ubiquitous, especially in the city centre around Piața Român.

◭ *The Ateneu Român provides a stunning setting for classical concerts*

International Women's Day on 8 March is a big event in Bucharest and the rest of Romania. It's traditional to make a gift of flowers to all the women in your life.

The biggest event of the spring is **Orthodox Easter**, which usually falls two weeks after the Roman equivalent. Easter is a bigger deal than Christmas in Romania, and many locals – even the young – still keep Lenten vows and attend Easter mass (always held at midnight on Easter Saturday).

May Day is traditionally celebrated either with an outing to the Black Sea coast (regardless of the weather) or by having a barbecue in one of the forests that surround the city, such as Baneasa.

Summer
Churches and monasteries are packed on 15 August as Romanians celebrate the Heavenly Birthday of the **Virgin Mary**.

In September, the **George Enescu Music Festival** at the Ateneu Român celebrates the life and work of Romania's greatest composer, George Enescu, and attracts some of the world's finest musicians.

Autumn
St Dumitru cel Nou (St Dumitru the New) is the patron saint of Bucharest, and is celebrated on 26 October when thousands of people queue at the Patriarchal Cathedral to view his remains.

Winter

Romania's national holiday is on 1 December and celebrates the unification of Transylvania with Wallachia and Moldavia in 1918. It is marked with a military parade in front of the Parliament Palace.

Christmas is a quiet time in Bucharest, as many of the city's residents go 'home' to their traditional villages or towns. They all come back for **New Year's Eve**, however; the biggest free party of the year is given by private television station Pro TV in Piața Revoluției, where live bands play from around 8pm to 4am.

January and February are the main months of the **skiing season**, although the upper slopes at Sinaia can often have snow well into May.

PUBLIC HOLIDAYS

To the chagrin of its workforce, Romania has precious few public holidays. While most shops, banks and businesses close, public transport continues to run, even on Christmas Day. Restaurants, cafés and bars are usually unaffected, except on Christmas Day, New Year's Day and Easter Sunday, when the city shuts down.

New Year's Day 1 Jan
Easter Apr/May
May Day 1 May
National Day 1 Dec
Christmas Day 25 Dec

The swagger returns

Bucharest had a vibrancy – despite or perhaps even because of the political ambivalence of the times – that went unmatched until a decade ago when, after years of darkness, the city began to recover its swagger. And just as the 1920s and 1930s were marked by the erection of glittering examples of interwar architecture that remain startling in their impact today (none more so than the Ambasador Hotel, see page 38), so the current period of economic growth has seen the construction of bold, confident examples of contemporary architecture. The finest current example of this is the daring Architectural Union building on Piața Revoluției (see page 67).

Yet just as the plethora of glorious architecture that made Bucharest popular in the interwar years did not seal its status as one of Europe's great cities, so the contemporary boom looks unlikely to do so. It is with this in mind that Bucharest's current administration, led by Mayor Adrian Viideanu, has set about reviving the city's historic, neglected centre, around Lipscani. Almost every street in this area is lined with glorious secession architecture, mainly town houses built in art nouveau style at the turn of the 20th century. Most are dilapidated, in many cases occupied illegally, and in need of careful, painstaking renovation. This will happen over many years (the first step was to pedestrianise the whole area, which happened early in 2006), but the fact that the city now has a plan in place to create what will be a living museum of historic importance is just another sign that Bucharest is about to hit the big time.

⬤ *The innovative Architectural Union building*

History

According to the legend, Bucharest was founded by a shepherd called Bucur, who set down to rest somewhere close to Piaţa Obor in the 12th century, liked the look of the place and created a city.

The city only really grew after Vlad III Ţepeş (Vlad III the Impaler) moved his princely court here in 1459. The city was partially burnt down by the Turks in the 16th century, but it grew again in the early 18th century around the current Lipscani district, which became the busiest trading post in Wallachia.

Occupied by Russians and Austrians for brief periods in the 19th century, Bucharest became the capital of the United Romanian Principalities of Wallachia and Moldavia in 1861, and by 1900 it had a population of 300,000, making it one of Europe's biggest cities. It remained the Romanian capital at the end of World War I (in which Romania fought with the Entente) after Transylvania was united with the principalities.

Romania was split during World War II. Most of Transylvania was awarded to Hungary under the terms of the Molotov-Ribbentrop Pact, while the rest of the country became a quasi-German protectorate. Romanian forces fought with the Nazis on the Eastern Front, and were involved in some of the war's more infamous massacres of Jews, the Odessa Massacre of 1941 included.

Wartime leader Ion Antonescu was arrested by the young king, Mihai, on 23 August 1944, and Romania immediately pulled out of the war. That did not prevent a Soviet invasion, and by 1947 the king had been forced to abdicate and a Stalinist regime installed. The 1950s were marked by subservience to Moscow.

After a slight thaw following the election of Nicolae Ceaușescu to head the Communist Party in 1965, the economy collapsed in the 1970s and 1980s, and repression grew. In December 1989 the population exploded in revolution, toppled Ceaușescu and heralded in a new government. The revolution was quickly hijacked by Ion Iliescu, a former henchman of Ceaușescu, who kept most power in his and his party's hands. Students demonstrating against the apparent replacement of one dictatorship with another were brutally killed by miners – staunch Iliescu loyalists – in Piața Universității in June 1990.

Since then Bucharest has been slowly transformed into a modern European capital. Iliescu left the presidency for good in 2004, and most remnants of the old regime left with him. The government that replaced him has overseen an incredible amount of reform, culminating in the country's accession to the EU on 1 January 2007.

🔵 *The Central Committee building's balcony, site of Ceaușescu's last speech*

Lifestyle

On the surface, Bucharest is just like any other European capital. The same brand names tout their wares in bright lights from city-centre rooftops, the city's young population shamelessly flaunts its new-found attitude or wealth, and expensive cars park haphazardly on pavements with utter disregard for passers-by.

Underneath, however, Bucharest is different. Even the bright young things zooming the city's streets on their trendy mopeds have vague recollections of the recent past, when queuing for basic foodstuffs was a day-to-day activity. The legacy of those days most visible in today's young Bucharest buck is the need to do everything instantly; why live for tomorrow? It is this that in many ways gives the city its dynamism. Do not be surprised then that Bucharest's young people may appear to have little time for the questions and enquiries of bewildered travellers; they are not being rude, that's just the way they are.

The older generation – for whom the memories of communism are far more vivid – gets the past out of its system in a different way. Smart enough to know that time changes nothing, they do nothing instantly, and leave everything for tomorrow. As this generation still has a monopoly in a number of the service professions, expect customer service to be – by and large – poor, if it exists at all.

One thing you cannot fail to notice while in town is the devoutness of Romanians of all ages. Look out for the cross the majority of Romanians make when passing a church, be it on foot, in a car or on public transport. Look out for the number of shops selling religious icons, and then for the nationality of the customers; they are not tourists, they're locals. The Romanian Orthodox Church (to which the vast majority of the city's population belongs) had a strange accommodation with the communist regime, but by hook or by crook its reputation survived intact. Since the revolution it has once again become the institution in the country that all age groups most trust and respect. Visiting at any time will give you a sense of this; visiting at Christmas or (especially) Easter will make you feel part of it.

⬤ Bucharest's young people taking time out

Culture

Even during the darker years of the communist regime, Bucharest's theatres were full, though fuel shortages meant they often went unheated. The city boasts no fewer than 25 working theatres, all with their own unique theatre companies; most are still supported by the state. The city's National Theatre is one of the city's landmarks; sitting in Piaţa Universităţii, its main hall is used for staging everything from musicals to serious drama. As it's all performed in Romanian, however, it is unlikely to tempt the visitor unless he or she is desperate to see *King Lear* in a foreign language. Instead, admire its strange exterior and head for the lively music venue it hosts on the top floor, Laptaria lui Enache, where good young bands of all descriptions play most nights.

More likely to be of interest to you is the Romanian National Opera, housed in a fine neoclassical building on Bulevardul Mihai Kogalniceanu. There are performances every day at 18.30, and tickets are cheap. The ballet shares the building, and one performance a week is usually reserved for ballet fans.

Bucharest has recently provided the backdrop for a number of big money Hollywood films. The high quality but low budget production facilities at the former state-run studios out at Buftea, along with cheap extras and skilled film technicians, have made film one of the city's most lucrative industries. Romanians in turn love the cinema, and the city boasts two huge multi-screen cinemas. The good news for visitors is that in Bucharest, films are shown in the original language with Romanian subtitles. Ticket prices are again extremely cheap.

◇ *The neoclassical façade of the National Theatre*

Bucharest is also becoming something of a Mecca for lovers of art deco architecture. It seems that even in the most depressing of side streets, the glorious, often faded grandeur of a 1920s masterpiece is ready to jump out at you. Bulevardul Magheru is home to a number of these gems; admire the two typical art deco hotels that stand opposite each other, the Lido and the Ambasador.

You will also find that there is no shortage of bookshops in the city. Romanians read more books than almost any other nation on earth, devouring all sorts of work by their own gifted authors, as well as an increasing amount of translated work by foreign writers. There are a growing number of decent English bookshops too; try Salingers at the Marriott hotel or the Libraria Dalles on Bulevardul Bălcescu. The crazy, chaotic streets of Lipscani also offer hidden first editions in its antique and pawn shops.

Row your cares away on the Cișmigiu Garden Lake

MAKING THE MOST OF
Bucharest

Shopping

If you are coming to Bucharest to shop, think again. You will find little here you can't get at home, and usually you'll pay more money here. Brand names that would be considered middle-of-the-road in Western Europe are luxury in Bucharest and priced accordingly.

What you do find in Bucharest, however, is a delightful range of antique shops, as well as plenty of specialist places selling unique gifts, such as Romanian Orthodox iconography, glass, naïve art and both communist and Nazi-era memorabilia. If a Lenin badge or statuette is what takes your fancy, you'll love Obor Market or the many antique shops of Lipscani.

The city's main shopping areas are Bulevardul Magheru and Calea Victoriei, where you will find high-end fashion labels, expensive boutiques and a bevy of perfumeries. Two modern malls now compete to attract the city's shoppers: București Mall (the first to open, back in 1999) and the larger and newer Plaza Romania. Both have big supermarkets, a range of fashion and electronics stores, children's shops and play areas, cinemas and vast food courts. The city's young people treat them as general meeting areas, and they are always full.

Piața Amzei is the city's main produce market, but there are others at Piața Obor and Piața Dorobanților. They mainly sell fresh fruit and vegetables but Obor especially can become something of a flea market at weekends.

If you want to take home something exclusively Romanian as a gift or souvenir, you could do worse than the Romanian version of Monopoly, on sale in most of the city's toy shops.

⬥ The main shopping street of Calea Victoriei

You could also go for some Romanian music; the operas and concertos of George Enescu, or some *muzica lautareasca*, as heard at weddings, christenings and parties all over Romania. Look out for CDs by Maria Dragomiroiu and Benone Sinulescu.

Up in Sinaia, the resort's ski shops offer cut-price skis and snowboards from mid-February onwards. Also look out for the craft markets that line the road between Sinaia, Bușteni and Azuga; most of the wares on offer are touristy rubbish, but there are choice goods too, including hand-woven lace, wooden children's toys and strangely fetching hand-knitted shepherds' pullovers.

USEFUL SHOPPING PHRASES

How much is this?
Cât costă?
Cuht costah?

Can I try this on?
Pot să o (îl) probez?
Pot sah oh (ul) probez?

My size is ...
Am mărimea ...
Mooy roz-myarh toh ...

I'll take this one, thank you
Oh iau pe aceasta, mulțumesc
Oh iaoo peh acheyasta, mooltzoomesc?

Eating & drinking

Good food in Bucharest is now thankfully very easy to find. In fact, choosing from the plethora of great, good-value eateries will be one of your hardest daily decisions while in town. Every genre is on offer, from traditional Romanian cuisine to cutting-edge fusion, and everything in between.

FOOD

Romanian food is tasty if unadventurous. Most restaurants serving local specialities will offer you a range of sour soups, known as *ciorbă*, which are full of vegetables and often meals in themselves. *Ciorbă de perisoare* (meatball sour soup) is particularly tasty, though *ciorbă de fasole* (bean sour soup) and *ciorbă de vacuţa* (beef sour soup) are also to be recommended. More of an acquired taste is the local favourite, *ciorbă de burta*, made from cows' intestines. After a *ciorbă* try some *sarmale* (cabbage leaves, or sometimes vine leaves, stuffed with meat

PRICE RATING
The following approximate price bands are based on the average cost of a three-course meal for one person, excluding drinks, and are indicated by these symbols:
£ under 50 lei   **££** 50–100 lei
£££ over 100 lei
In even the most expensive restaurants you will be hard pushed to spend more than 150 lei for a good meal, providing you do not go mad with the imported wines.

and rice) served with *mamaliga* (polenta) and covered in sour cream. It is the national dish. Romanians are also fond of large chunks of meat, such as *ciolan afumat* (pork knuckle) and *costițe* (ribs). Pork and chicken are the staples of the diet, with beef rarely found on menus (except in soups), while lamb is eaten only at Easter. *Mici* (mutton and beef meatballs served with mustard), however, are served in most restaurants and are wonderful, but always best when bought from a street stall. Fish is a disappointment here; expect to find trout, carp and perch on menus, but little else.

When it comes to dessert Romanians have very sweet tastes. Look out for *papanași* (dense little doughnuts covered in cream

🔺 *Don't miss out on a warming bowl of* ciorbă *(sour soup)*

and syrup) and *clatite* (pancakes) served piping hot with jam or chocolate. Snacks in Bucharest are found on street corners everywhere; look out for *covrigi* (sweet bread bagels covered in salt). They are delicious when hot.

DRINKS

There is no shortage of places to drink in Bucharest, from sophisticated cafés and tea houses to cocktail bars and Irish pubs. Coffee in Romania is very good, though tea usually means herbal varieties. Make sure you ask for *ceai negru* if you want a black tea, and *cu lapte* if you want it with milk.

The local spirit is *țuica*, a highly distilled aperitif made from grapes or prunes, incredibly strong and an acquired taste. For a

EATING OUT

Standards of service can vary, and it is not uncommon to be entirely ignored by staff after taking your seat. Be explicit about what exactly you want (confusions occur often), but don't be surprised if your chosen dish is not available, even in the best restaurants. A 10 per cent tip is expected, whether deserved or not, but you will be doing Romania a disservice by handing out a tip when it has not been well earned. If you'd rather avoid the hassle and just sit outdoors with a sandwich, be warned: picnicking in one of the city's parks will probably get you arrested (in most parks ideal grassy picnic spots are off limits). Should you wish to eat on the move, you can pick up picnic supplies in the city's supermarkets or *alimentară* stores.

more satisfying taste of Romania try some of the country's excellent wines. Familiar red grapes such as Merlot and Cabernet Sauvignon have a great tradition in Romania, though quality and price are directly linked; pay as much as you can. White wines are less impressive, though anything on the Chateau Domenii label is worthwhile. You may also like to try the sweet sparkling wine from the Cricova winery in Moldova. Local beer is cheap and good (look out for the Timisoreana, Aurora and Ciucas brands especially), though is losing market share among the city's young folk to imported Danish, German, Belgian and Czech beers.

USEFUL DINING PHRASES

I'd like a table for ... people
Doresc o masă pentru ... persoane
Po-pro-shair o sto-leek dla ... o-soob

Waiter!
Chelner/Chelneriță!
Kelner/Kelnehritsa!

Does this contain meat?
Conține carne?
Kontzyneh carneh?

Could I have the bill please?
Nota de plată, vă rog?
Notah deh platah, vah rohg?

Where is the toilet, please?
Unde este toaleta, vă rog?
Oondeh este twaleta, vah rohg?

Entertainment & nightlife

There is no longer any doubt that Bucharest is now well and truly on the European clubbing map. The biggest-name DJs in the world play the city's trendiest clubs at least once a week, with the gigs of the very biggest names on the decks taking place outdoors in summer, or in the enormous Romexpo exhibition centre in winter. Kristal Glam Club started it all off around 2000, paying real money to bring over the biggest names. Now three venues (Kristal, Studio Martin and Bamboo) all compete for the affections of the city's clubbers. Tickets are rarely sold in advance, and it's first come first served on the door at the venues; get there early. Sometimes, for the very biggest names, it is possible to pre-book tickets. Look out for details in *Bucharest In Your Pocket* (see page 33) or try the website Ⓦ www.bilete.ro

It isn't all good news for music lovers though. While the club scene raves itself onto the European hot list, Bucharest is still given a wide berth by top performers. Occasionally a genuine big name turns up, such as Michael Jackson in 1996 and Depeche Mode in 2006 (the biggest concert ever held in Romania), but by and large the city has to make do with has-beens looking for an easy pay day. For a taste of the local music scene, however, you might like to try a venue such as Club A (see page 88), which has concerts two or three nights a week. Again, tickets are usually sold at the door.

When it comes to more mainstream nightlife, the lack of a real city centre makes it difficult to identify the best place to find pubs, bars and clubs. A couple of quasi 'strips' have begun to appear, however, such as the string of cafés along the southern end of Strada Radu Beller at Piața Dorobanților, and Strada Mendeleev around Piața Amzei. The Radu Beller strip is especially popular in summer, when tables are placed in a haphazard and impromptu manner on the pavements outside.

◼ *Bucharest has earned its place on Europe's coolest clubbing list*

Bucharest is also now a major mover in the world of gambling. You can barely walk down a street in the centre of the city without passing a plush casino. Try the Grand Casinos at the Athénée Palace Hilton or the J W Marriott (see page 41), or the Casino Bucharest at the InterContinental (see page 41).

The other side of Bucharest's nightlife is its seedier, red light side. Note that despite all appearances prostitution is illegal in Romania, and though ladies of the night are a common sight around the city centre (especially the southern end of Calea Victoriei), you risk a heavy fine even by approaching them. Strip clubs are technically legal operations but note that many are merely fronts for unseemly activities and are best avoided.

LISTINGS

Whatever is going on in Bucharest, from concerts to exhibitions, club nights to new restaurant openings, you'll find details of it in one of three places: the indispensable English-language bi-monthly *Bucharest In Your Pocket*, available in good hotels, restaurants and expat hangouts all over the city; or the two heavily competing Romanian-language weeklies, *Şapte Seri* and *B24-FUN*. They both appear on Wednesday evenings and you can pick them up for free almost anywhere, from McDonald's to metro stations. Though the listings are in Romanian, the cinema schedule is easy enough to understand for even the most boorish of monoglots.

Sport & relaxation

SPECTATOR SPORTS

Football

The national sport is football. The biggest club in the city (and country for that matter) is Steaua Bucharest. The other two teams in the capital, Dinamo and Rapid, are less well supported, but derbies between any of the three are packed-out affairs well worth attending. Tickets are cheap and can be bought from the stadiums in advance of matches. The season runs from August to July, with a three-month break from December to March.

Steaua Bucharest ⓐ Complex Sportiv Steaua, B-dul Ghencea 45
ⓣ 021 411 56 56 ⓦ www.steauafc.com

Dinamo ⓐ Complex Sportiv Dinamo, Șos Ștefan cel Mare
ⓣ 021 210 69 74 ⓦ www.fcdinamo.ro

Rapid ⓐ Stadion Rapid, Șos Giulești ⓦ www.fcrapid.ro

Others

The three football clubs above all run teams in a number of other sports, and once again, derbies attract large crowds. **Basketball** games tend to be played at the Sala Polivalenta (ⓐ B-dul Tineretului), **ice hockey** at the national ice rink (ⓐ Patinoar din Complex Sportiv Lia Manoliu, B-dul Basarabiei) and **rugby** at mini-stadiums behind the football grounds (usually with free entrance). In September, the Romanian **Open Tennis Championships** are held at the National Tennis Centre (ⓐ Str Dr Lister).

For venues and ticket information for all sports, including football, check out the sports newspaper *Gazeta Sporturilor* (ⓦ www.gsp.ro).

PARTICIPATION SPORTS
Bowling
There are two bowling alleys in the city, one at the București Mall (📍 Calea Vitan 53–55 🕐 10.00–24.00), the other at the Plaza Romania (📍 B-dul Timișoara 26 🕐 10.00–23.00).

Horse-riding
Ecvahalis is a large equestrian centre. It's open all year round and inexpensive. You'll need to take a taxi there. 📍 Aleea Priveghitorilor 35 ☎ 021 315 28 77 🕐 07.00–18.30

Ice-skating
At the Lia Manoliu Rink you can hire rather old skates for around 30 lei. In winter you can skate alfresco on Cișmigiu Lake in Cișmigiu Garden. Skate hire is a little more expensive here.
Lia Manoliu Rink 📍 B-dul Basarabiei 37–39 ☎ 021 324 65 35 🕐 10.00–16.00 Mon–Sun, closed for big ice hockey matches. Admission charge

Skiing
Head to the resort of Sinaia in the winter for great, challenging skiing (see page 123).

Swimming
There is a large public indoor swimming pool at the Hotel Best Western Parc (📍 B-dul Poligrafiei 3–5 ☎ 021 549 20 00 🕐 10.00–22.00). In summer try the large and popular Water Park (📍 Șos București-Ploiești 🕐 10.00–20.00 🌐 www.waterpark.ro) opposite Henri Coanda Otopeni airport.

● Sinaia is a top skiing destination

Accommodation

Visitors to the city still tend to be mainly business travellers on expense accounts, and the choice at the sharp end of the market is far greater than at backpacker level. There is nowhere to camp in Bucharest, but there are hostels and a couple of cheap and cheerful bargain hotels. The mid-range market remains something of a void. Those reasonable 3-star places that do exist tend to be out of the city centre and quite often fail to reach international standards. You are best to spend as much as you can afford.

Note that most parts of Bucharest city centre are very busy and crowded with traffic. For a quiet sleep you are better off in one of the more serene districts, such as the north of the city, although you'll have the expense of taxis into the city centre.

Booking in advance is always a good idea, either through an internet hotel booking site or direct through the hotel. Avoid turning up on spec as you will end up paying the rack rate, which is always 30 per cent (or more) expensive than pre-booking. A buffet breakfast is almost always included in the

PRICE RATING

Note that almost all hotels in Bucharest, and throughout Romania, list their prices in euros (€). The following price guides indicate the approximate cost of a room for two people for one night, including breakfast, VAT and local taxes.

£ under €100   ££ €100–€150   £££ over €150

room rate. Tea and coffee facilities are usually not available in rooms, even in the best hotels. Cable television with at least one English news channel is standard in all but the cheapest places, and en suite bathrooms pretty much standard; expect a shower, however, not an actual bath tub. Most hotel staff speak good English.

HOTELS

Ambasador £ Though the somewhat stuffy rooms and services of the hotel inside do not match the fabulous art deco building, it has a great location and prices are relatively cheap. ⓐ B-dul Magheru 8–10 ① 021 315 90 80 ⑤ 021 312 35 95 ⓦ www.ambasador.ro ⓔ hotel@ambasador.ro

Cerna £ Clean, cheap but very small rooms close to the city's main railway station. En suite facilities and televisions cost extra. Great breakfast. ⓐ B-dul Dinicu Golescu 29 ① 021 311 05 35 ⑤ 021 311 07 21

Hanul lui Manuc £ The rooms at the Han are not luxurious, but for atmosphere they are hard to beat. Note that the Han – also a bar and restaurant – is busy throughout the day and night, and getting peace and quiet here is difficult. ⓐ Str Franceză 62–64 ① 021 313 14 11 ⑤ 021 312 28 11 ⓦ www.hanulmanuc.ro

Villa Helga £ Bucharest's only official Hostelling International affiliated hostel, this place offers the cheapest beds in the city, alongside a host of extras, from free breakfast to kitchen and laundry room access. No curfew. ⓐ Str Mihai Eminescu 184

☎ 021 312 08 28 ⓦ www.rotravel.com/hotels/ helga
ⓔ villa_helga@yahoo.com

El Greco ££ Housed inside a gorgeous neoclassical villa, an
exquisite hotel offering luxurious, large rooms at a decent (if not
exactly bargain) price. ⓐ Str Jean Louis Calderon 16 ☎ 021 315 81 31
🆔 021 315 88 98 ⓦ www.hotelelgreco.ro ⓔ office@hotelelgreco.ro

Golden Tulip ££ Just north of Piaţa Revoluţiei, this 4-star hotel
offers free wireless internet in all its large rooms. A bit
characterless, it does have a well-equipped health club, with
sauna and whirlpool. ⓐ Calea Victoriei 166 ☎ 021 212 55 58
🆔 021 212 51 21 ⓦ www.goldentulipbucharest.com
ⓔ office@goldentulipbucharest.com

Opera ££ Good mid-range choice, but noisily close to Piaţa
Revoluţiei. The winding staircase up to the rooms is a gem, and
the small, garishly decorated but well-appointed rooms are
good value. ⓐ Str Ion Brezoianu 37 ☎ 021 312 48 55
🆔 021 312 48 58 ⓦ www.hotelopera.ro ⓔ info@hotelopera.ro

Rembrandt ££ Best-value place in the city. Great little rooms, all
individually furnished with style and panache. Run by friendly
Dutch people and with a perfect location in Lipscani. ⓐ Str
Smardan 11 ☎ 021 313 93 15 🆔 021 313 93 15
ⓦ www.rembrandt.ro ⓔ info@rembrandt.ro

K&K Elisabeta ££–£££ The Czech Koller brothers' latest hotel, it's
a stunning villa conversion in the city centre. Expect the usual

K&K extras, from personal service to antique furniture.
ⓐ Str Slanic 26 ☎ 021 311 86 31 🖷 021 311 86 32
🌐 www.kkhotels.co.ro ⓔ hotel.elisabeta@kkhotels.co.ro

Novotel City Centre ££–£££ The charm is provided by the
entrance, an exact replica of the National Theatre, which stood
on the site until bombed by the British in World War II.
Modernity and gadgets aplenty inside. Friendly staff and a
sensational location make the price worthwhile. ⓐ Calea Victoriei
37B ☎ 021 312 51 14 🖷 021 313 11 37 🌐 www.novotel.com
ⓔ H5558@accor.com

● The welcoming and homely Rembrandt hotel

Athénée Palace Hilton £££ Unquestionably the best hotel in the city, it affords luxury at every turn. The view from the rooms overlooking historic Piaţa Revoluţiei are worth the extra money they cost. Look out for special deals on the Hilton website. ⓐ Str Episcopiei 1–3 ⓣ 021 303 37 77 ⓕ 021 315 38 13 ⓦ www.hilton.com ⓔ sales.bucharest@hilton.com

Crowne Plaza £££ The quiet setting away from the city centre makes this a good choice for families. Luxurious rooms, outstanding service and excellent Sunday brunch. ⓐ B-dul Poligrafiei 1 ⓣ 021 224 00 34 ⓕ 021 318 13 02 ⓦ www.bucharest.crowneplaza.com ⓔ reservations@crowneplaza.ro

InterContinental £££ For almost three decades the only 5-star hotel in the city. From its balconies journalists reported live on the revolution taking place below in December 1989. ⓐ B-dul Nicolae Bălcescu 2–4 ⓣ 021 310 20 20 ⓕ 021 312 04 86 ⓦ www.intercontinental.com ⓔ buchareat@interconti.ro

J W Marriott £££ The preferred choice of businessmen for its superb business facilities. ⓐ Calea 13 Septembrie 90 ⓣ 021 403 10 00 ⓕ 021 403 10 01 ⓦ www.jwmarriott.ro ⓔ mhrs.buhro.marketing.asst@marriotthotels.com

Sofitel £££ Unsurpassed on-site amenities and large rooms, though less luxurious than you may expect. ⓐ P-ta Montreal 10 ⓣ 021 318 30 00 ⓕ 021 316 25 50 ⓦ www.sofitel.com ⓔ reservation@sofitel.ro

THE BEST OF BUCHAREST

Bucharest offers a surprising mix of fascinating museums, grand palaces and unusual architecture. You can kick back in one of the tranquil parks, or just sit with a coffee and take in the city's vibrant atmosphere.

TOP 10 ATTRACTIONS

- **Casa Poporului** Ceaușescu's folly; reputedly the second-biggest building in the world (see page 76).

- **Muzeul Satului (Village Museum)** An open-air museum showcasing the best of the architecture of the Romanian countryside (see page 97).

- **Muzeul Țăranului Român (Peasant Museum)** Bucharest's best museum hosts fascinating exhibitions and organises craft and arts workshops (see page 97).

- **Herăstrău Park** Bucharest's largest park with lakes, paths, playgrounds, cafés and terraces (see page 94).

- **Skating on frozen Cişmigiu Garden Lake** Hire yourself some skates and join in, or buy a glass of hot wine and sit back and admire the accomplished performers on the ice (see page 64).

- **Muzeul Naţional de Artă (National Art Museum)** All of Romania's best-known artists have work exhibited here, from painter Nicolae Grigorescu to sculptor Constantin Brâncuşi (see page 69).

- **Curtea Veche (Old Court Church & Palace)** Bucharest first developed as a city around the 15th-century court palace, now no more than ruins (see page 82).

- **Athénée Palace Bistro & Terrace** Since the 1920s the great and good have drunk coffee here and watched the world go by (see page 60).

- **Muzeul de Istorie al Evreilor din România (Jewish History Museum)** Half of Romania's Jews died in the Holocaust. This museum commemorates them (see page 83).

- *Covrigi* If you're lucky enough to get a piping hot one, you will be hooked for life on these simple but tasty bagels (see page 29).

⬤ *Dazzling frescoes in the Radu Vodă Monastery*

HALF-DAY: BUCHAREST IN A HURRY

You'll have enough time to whizz around Casa Poporului and to
see the main sights of the city centre on foot. Start at the Casa
Poporului and join the tour of the building. Walk along
Bulevardul Unirii to the enormous Piața Unirii, taking a left
towards the Hanul lui Manuc. You should be able to squeeze in
a quick coffee in the café on the ground floor. Behind the Hanul
are the remains of the Princely Court, the city's oldest buildings.
A short walk uphill past the Old Court Church brings you to the
lovely jumble of old shops that is Lipscani. Pass the National
Bank and head for the onion-domed Russian Church. Just ahead
is the main building of Bucharest University and the historically
important Piața Universității.

1 DAY: TIME TO SEE A LITTLE MORE

After following the half-day itinerary, having allowed a little
more time for browsing the antique shops of Lipscani and
popping in to the Hanul cu Tei, take a walk north from Piața
Universității along Bulevardul Magheru, paying special
attention to the glorious art deco architecture of the Lido and
Ambasador hotels. Turn left as you pass the Lido, and head for
Piața Revoluției. After an outdoor lunch at Café & Terrace,
admire the abstract revolution monument and spend an hour in
the National Art Museum. The collection of religious art on the
first floor is the main attraction here. You'll then need to hail a
cab to the enchantingly non-urban Village Museum. Head next
door to Herăstrău Park to enjoy the host of terraces and
restaurants on the shore of Lake Herăstrău.

2–3 DAYS: SHORT CITY BREAK

The extra time would allow you to enjoy the suggestions opposite in a more leisurely manner, then fit in visits to the Peasant Museum, the Jewish Museum and Cișmigiu Garden. The Botanical Gardens are a half-day trip in themselves, while Lake Snagov and Mogosoia Palace are full-day trips, including a picnic or barbecue lunch. At night make sure you sample the city's top restaurants and bars.

LONGER: ENJOYING BUCHAREST TO THE FULL

You can do all the above and still have time to experience the full Top 10 Attractions list. One entire day can be spent just enjoying the bustle and life of the city centre, browsing the shops of Magheru and Calea Victoriei. There will also be the chance to head out to Sinaia for a day or two's skiing or mountain walking (depending on the time of year), and to visit the Sinaia Monastery and Peleș Castle.

● Wander through the historical Lipscani district

Something for nothing

All of Bucharest's churches are free to enter, though all have
small donation boxes at the entrance; just give what you can.
Another way of donating something is to do as the locals do,
and buy a candle and light it for the memory of a loved one.
The best churches are the Kretulescu Church on Piața Revoluției,
which was recently fully renovated inside and out, and the tiny
but gorgeous Small White Church close by on Calea Victoriei.
A little further away is the Russian Church on Strada Ion Ghica,
whose onion domes are a feature of the city. Back on Piața
Revoluției it costs nothing to go inside the Ateneu and to
admire its fine lobby, while the National Art Museum opposite
is free on the first Wednesday of every month. For glorious free
views of the communist-era city centre, take the lift or
escalators to the top floor of the Unirea department store on
Piața Unirii.

All of Bucharest's parks and green spaces (except the
Botanical Gardens) are free, and the well-kept gardens and
paths of Cișmigiu Garden make it a great place to escape the
city bustle and take a rest on one of its characteristic green
benches. If you are a decent chess player you can challenge the
experts who congregate here from dawn to dusk, regardless of
the weather. Be warned though, the standard is high!

For a taste of the real Romania, head for the enormous Piața
Obor to the east of the city centre, where all kinds of life, from
card sharks to Gypsies in full traditional, colourful regalia,
congregate. You will find everything imaginable on sale here,
from fresh fruit and vegetables to spare parts for old Romanian

cars long out of production. The real fun though is watching real Romanians living real lives, such as old women haggling over the price of potatoes, or taking part in mini-auctions of live chickens and ducks. For maximum effect come in the morning when the market is at its busiest.

⬥ *Enjoy the National Art Museum's treasures, once a month for free*

When it rains

There is no getting away from the fact that Bucharest is miserable when it rains. Though all of the churches and museums can be visited in a shower, they are some distance away from each other. Walking the city can be unpleasant as its poor drainage system means that water sits on the road surface, making some streets – even in the city centre – impassable for pedestrians (unless you want very wet feet) after the merest of downpours. You'll therefore be constantly calling taxis, so try and head for places that can fill up more than an hour or two at a time; the Casa Poporului, the Peasant Museum and the National Art Museum are good choices.

Another suggestion is a visit to one of the city's two big shopping malls, the București Mall or the Plaza Romania. Both have multi-screen cinemas, bowling alleys, children's play areas, a choice of cafés and restaurants and enough shops to keep you happy for a wet morning or afternoon.

If you get caught in a shower while in the city centre and a cab will not stop, dive into somewhere such as Cremcaffé (see page 87) or the English bar at the Hilton (see page 74), where you will be able to spend a couple of glorious hours drinking coffee (or something stronger) and reading newspapers (provided) in a variety of languages.

Further suggestions for rainy days include swimming (see page 35), or try a game of indoor golf at the City Swing Club (ⓐ Str Ștefan Mihaileanu 20 ⓣ 021 327 94 64 ⓦ www.cityswing.ro), whose golf simulators offer you the chance to try a round on one of 20 well-known international courses.

⬤ Choose a drizzly day to lose yourself inside the Casa Poporului

On arrival

TIME DIFFERENCES

Bucharest is two hours ahead of Greenwich Mean Time (GMT). At 12.00 in Bucharest, times elsewhere are as follows:

Australia EST 19.00, CST 18.30, WST 17.00

New Zealand 21.00

South Africa 11.00

UK 10.00

USA & Canada Newfoundland 06.30, Atlantic Canada 06.00, Eastern 05.00, Central 04.00, Mountain 03.00, Pacific 02.00, Alaska 01.00

ARRIVING

By air

Bucharest has two international airports. If you arrive by scheduled flight with a state-owned airline or with Romania's national airline, Tarom, you will land at **Henri Coanda Otopeni International Airport**, 17 km (10½ miles) from the city centre. It's small but has all the basic facilities: ATMs, bureaux de change (which should be avoided due to their high commission), car hire, cafés and reliable taxis. Avoid the taxi touts at the exit, and head instead for the blue and grey Fly Taxi people carriers that sit outside the arrivals terminal. A ride to the city centre will cost around 100 lei (€27). A cheaper option is to take the airport bus 783 that stops underneath the arrivals hall, in front of the domestic flight terminal. Tickets cost around 5 lei and are valid for the return journey too. Buy them in the silver kiosk next to the bus stop before boarding. The bus runs from around

05.30 to 22.30 and stops at Piața Victoriei, Piața Romana and Piața Universității, terminating at Piața Unirii.

Bucharest's second airport is **Aurel Vlaicu International Airport**, 10 km (6 miles) from the city centre. It is used mainly by budget airlines and is basic. There is an ATM, however, though no car hire desks. Bus 133 to Piața Romana is the best way to get into town. Tickets cost around 1 lei and need to be bought from the kiosks opposite the airport before boarding, then stamped once on the bus (see page 55).

By train

Gara de Nord (☎ 021 9521 ⬤ www.cfr.ro) is an exact replica – on the outside – of the more famous Gare du Nord in Paris, and is the only station in the city travellers are ever likely to use. It has left luggage (🕐 06.00–24.00), ATMs, a café, a McDonald's (🕐 07.00–24.00), newsstands and a shop selling the foreign

⬤ The towering InterContinental hotel is a useful landmark

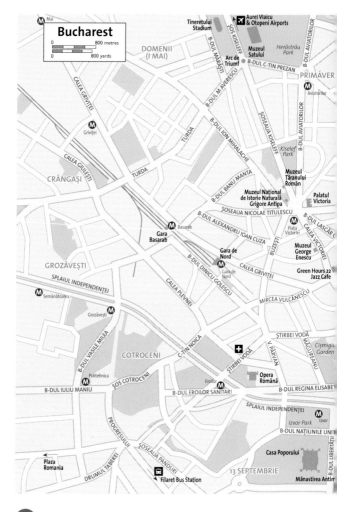

press. Taxis wait outside, but read the advice on Bucharest's taxis first (page 58). The city centre is also accessible by the metro system: Piața Victoriei is a short ride (two stations) from Gara de Nord on metro line M1. And trolleybus 85 runs from outside the station to Piața Universității.

By bus
Filaret Bus Station (ⓐ Piața Garii Filaret 1 ⓣ 021 336 06 92 ⓦ www.autogari.ro) is east of the city centre and has no ATM or left luggage or much of anything else. The only way to get to the city centre from Filaret is to chance a taxi or catch bus 232 to Piața Unirii (if the kiosk selling bus tickets is open).

FINDING YOUR FEET
Bucharest is a remarkably safe city. The biggest dangers to pedestrians are posed by drivers disregarding road rules, and the city's population of around 75,000 street dogs (see page 132). While major boulevards and streets are clearly signposted, side streets can go entirely unmarked. The numbering of buildings also leaves a lot to be desired, so a good map is useful.

ORIENTATION
Bucharest's biggest problem for tourists is that it lacks a single, genuine city centre; Piața Universității, Piața Unirii and Piața Romana all compete for that title. The best focal point is probably Piața Universității, as its InterContinental hotel is visible from much of the city. As a guide, keep a mental note of where you are in relation to Calea Victoriei, the city's main north–south thoroughfare.

GETTING AROUND
Buses, trolleybuses & trams

Bucharest has recently invested heavily in buses, and most lines through the city centre are now served by modern, wide buses. They are still overcrowded, however, and have no air conditioning in summer. The city also has a network of trams and trolleybuses, but they are painfully slow and only skirt the city centre. In fact, most tourists tend to avoid public transport altogether – taxis are so cheap in Bucharest that even the most penny-pinching backpacker can afford them. However, if you do wish to brave the buses, trams or trolleybuses, the ticketing system for all three is the same; you need to purchase a ticket from a silver kiosk marked *Bilete RATB* before boarding. Once on board frank the ticket in the contraptions attached to the vehicle. On-the-spot fines for being caught without a valid, franked ticket are high. Not all stops have ticket booths, so stock up when you get the chance.

IF YOU GET LOST, TRY ...

Do you speak English?	**Where is ...?**
Vobiți englezește?	Unde este ...?
Vorbeetz englezeshteh?	*Oondeh esteh ...?*

Can you point to it on my map?
Puteți să-mi arătați pe harta?
Pootetz sah-mee arahatz pe hartah?

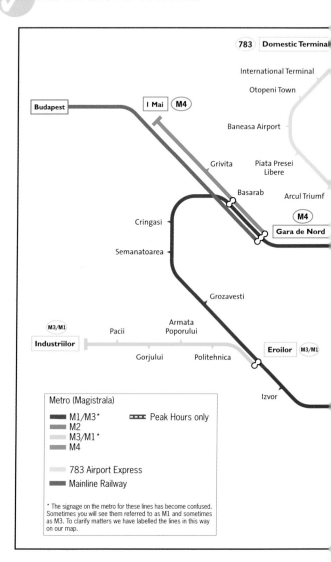

783 | Domestic Terminal

International Terminal

Otopeni Town

Budapest

I Mai | M4

Baneasa Airport

Grivita

Piata Presei Libere

Basarab

Arcul Triumf

M4

Gara de Nord

Cringasi

Semanatoarea

Grozavesti

Armata Poporului

M3/M1

Pacii

Industriilor

Gorjului

Politehnica

Eroilor | M3/M1

Izvor

Metro (Magistrala)

▬▬ M1/M3*
▬▬ M2
▬▬ M3/M1*
▬▬ M4

▭▭▭ Peak Hours only

▬▬ 783 Airport Express
▬▬ Mainline Railway

* The signage on the metro for these lines has become confused. Sometimes you will see them referred to as M1 and sometimes as M3. To clarify matters we have labelled the lines in this way on our map.

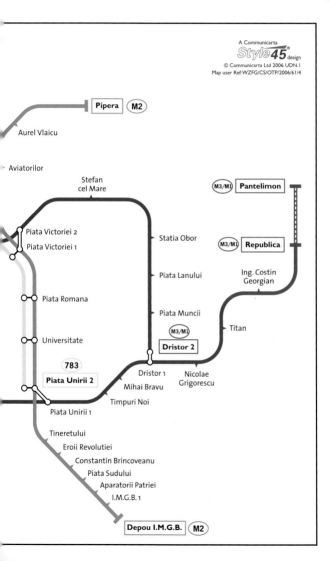

A Communicarta
Style 45 design
© Communicarta Ltd 2006 UDN.1
Map user Ref:WZFG/CS/OTP/2006/61/4

Pipera (M2)

Aurel Vlaicu

Aviatorilor

Stefan cel Mare

(M3/M1) Pantelimon

Piata Victoriei 2
Piata Victoriei 1

Statia Obor

(M3/M1) Republica

Piata Lanului

Ing. Costin Georgian

Piata Romana

Piata Muncii

(M3/M1)

Titan

Universitate

Dristor 2

783

Piata Unirii 2

Dristor 1   Nicolae Grigorescu
Mihai Bravu

Timpuri Noi

Piata Unirii 1

Tineretului
Eroii Revolutiei
Constantin Brincoveanu
Piata Sudului
Aparatorii Patriei
I.M.G.B. 1

Depou I.M.G.B. (M2)

Metro

Bucharest's relatively new metro system was built primarily to ship workers out to the huge industrial estates on the edge of the city. Only a couple of places in the city centre are served. Tickets are purchased at station entrances, and they need to be franked at the platform entrance.

Taxis

Most Bucharest taxis (all of which are painted yellow) are honest and cheap. Stick to a taxi from a trusted company (see below) and you will be OK. Problems are posed by unscrupulous privateers who overcharge. The good news is that tariffs have to be displayed on the taxi door. Do not pay more than about 2 lei (around €0.60) per kilometre (Fly Taxis charge more). Ensure the meter is running before setting off.

As ☎ 021 9435
Cristaxi ☎ 021 9461/6
Getax ☎ 021 9453
Meridian ☎ 021 9444
Perrozzi ☎ 021 9631

CAR HIRE

Car hire in Bucharest is now relatively cheap, though beware of hidden extras.

Avis Ⓦ www.avis.ro
Europcar Ⓦ www.ahl-autorent.ro
Hertz Ⓦ www.hertz.com.ro

▶ *The National Savings Bank is an architectural highlight*

Around Piața Revoluției

Piața Revoluției is where the primary events of the Romanian revolution took place, and it can in many ways be regarded as the soul of the city. It is the perfect place to begin exploring Bucharest. A large and open square, it straddles Calea Victoriei, the city's main north–south artery, and is surrounded by historic buildings on all sides, including the landmark Athénée Palace Hilton, the Ateneu Român concert hall, the former Royal Palace, the former Central Committee building, and the Humanitas bookstore, complete with bullet holes from those dramatic events of December 1989. A number of smart and pleasant side streets host boutiques and trendy restaurants, while the bustle of Piața Amzei, the city centre's biggest market, is a short walk north. A couple of hundred metres in the other direction is the far quieter Cișmigiu Garden, a genuine oasis of calm.

SIGHTS & ATTRACTIONS

Athénée Palace
So much has gone on in the 90 or so years since the Athénée Palace was opened that a former American diplomat, Rosie Waldeck, based in Bucharest during World War II, wrote a book – *Athene Palace* – about the intrigues, espionage and double dealings that went on here throughout the 1930s and 1940s. At the time this was the only luxury hotel in the city, and anyone of any importance who came to Bucharest stayed here. The building itself, though much renovated since its completion in 1912, retains its original late secession profile – note the

ironwork of the balconies – with some early art deco squiggles added later. Inside, the lobby is neoclassical, with marble columns and a sublime ballroom. If there are no events going on, the staff allow visitors to take a look round. Keep an eye out for the sepia photos placed all over the building showing how various sections and rooms looked half a century ago. Top your visit off with a sharp one at the English Bar; it's open to non-guests and retains its original layout, with high-back leather chairs and comfortable sofas. The bar features heavily in Olivia Manning's *Balkan Trilogy*.

ⓐ Piaţa Revoluţiei/Str Episcopiei 1–3

⬤ *The Athénée Palace hotel is a living vestige of Bucharest's history*

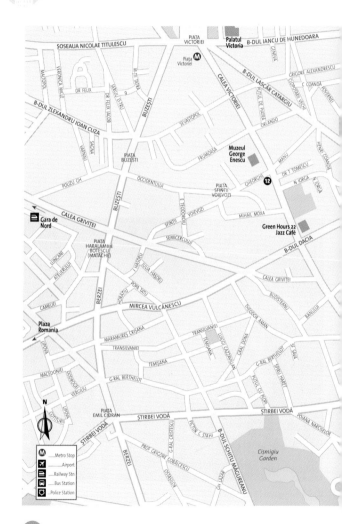

Around Piaţa Revoluţiei

0   400 metres

0   400 yards

Ştefan cel Mare

D EMMANUEL
C PETRESCU
ION BOCDAN
POLONA
CALEA DOROBANŢILOR
SLATINEANU
CRACIUN
VODE CARAGEA
JUIA
FIERARI
RASPANTILOR
AUREL VLAICU
FECIOAREI
TUNARI
DOGARILOR
BELDICEANU
SLAVEŞTI
DOLL CALUN ION
C-TIN DANIEL
VISARION
BASTILEI
STANISLAV CHIOCHIU
GIURESCU
G-RAL ERNEST BROSTEANU
POLONA
EMINESCU
MACEDONSKI
MIHAI
ALEXANDRU FILIPIDE
ALECU RUSSO
PIAŢA
ROMANA
URALI
B-DUL DACIA
DROBETA
PIAŢA
ROMANA
PIAŢA
SPANIEI
OBRESCU D
PIAŢA
A LAHOVARI
EREMIA GRIGORESCU
Ioanid
Park
GH IOANID
POLONA
DUMBRAVA ROŞIE
AUREL VLAICU
NEGRU
18
HENRI COANDA
B-DUL G-RAL GH MAGHERU
TACHE IONESCU
LITEUSI
COLUMB
PIAŢA GH
CANTACUZINO
11
BISERICA AMZEI
3
13
TACHE IONESCU
J MICHELET
DIONISIE LUPU
PITAR MOS
Ioanid
Garden
JEAN
ICOANEI
VERONA
SCHITU DARVARI
PIAŢA
AMZEI
GEORGE ENESCU
PICTOR
LOUIS
I L CARAGIALE
M ROSETTI
SPIRIDON JS
KRETULESCU
CALEA VICTORIEI
Athénée
Palace
hotel
4
14
NICOLAE GOLESCU
9
EXARCU
FRANKLIN
6
8
Ateneu
Român
C A ROSETTI
C A ROSETTI
SCOALEI
THOMAS MASARIK
I L CARAGIALE
G CLEMENCEA
B-DUL ALEX
7
1
PIAŢA
G ENESCU
C A ROSETTI
5
ROMANI
2
I DOBRESCU
NICOLAE FILIPESCU
LIDKA
C-RAL BUDIŞTEANU
CALDERON
BATIŞTEI
BACAROGU
OTTETI
eul Naţional
de Artă
B-DUL N BALCESCU
TRAIAN VUIA
BLANDUZIE
ITALIANĂ
Royal
Palace
VENUS A
DIANEI
Sala
Palatului
PIAŢA
G REVOLUŢIEI
Senate
(Former Central
Committee building)
IOTHERII
BATIŞTEI
ARGHEZI
JEAN LOUIS CALDERON
V LASCAR
SPERANTEI C NICO
Biserica
Creţulescu
Bucureşti
Mall
Teatru
Naţional
ION CAMPINEANU
ION CAMPINEANU

Fosta Cladire a Comitetului Central al Partidului Comunist Român (Former Central Committee Building)

It was from the balcony of this enormous 1950s building, constructed to house the Communist Party Central Committee, that communist dictator Nicolae Ceaușescu made his last public speech to the Romanian people on 21 December 1989. He fled with his wife the next day by helicopter from the roof as revolutionaries ransacked the lower floors. After the revolution and the disbandment of the Communist Party the building served for over a decade as the Romanian Senate, but since that body moved to the Casa Poporului in 2004 it has stood more or less empty. It is closed to the public.

🅐 Piața Revoluției

Grădina Cișmigiu (Cișmigiu Garden)

Though invariably referred to as Cișmigiu Park, this is officially a garden, laid out to the designs of Austrian landscape artist Carl Meyer from 1845 to 1860. Meyer brought in more than 30,000 trees, plants and shrubs from all over Romania to showcase the diverse flora of the country. Cișmigiu is busy all day every day; its long gladed walkways provide a superb backdrop for strollers. On weekends the place truly buzzes, with the yelps and screams of the children's playgrounds alongside the contented murmurs of quieter pursuits such as chess, or rowing on the artificial lake. The lake is frozen in winter and becomes a natural ice rink; skate hire is available. Throughout the year numerous terraces and cafés serve coffee, drinks and cakes.

🅐 Between B-dul Regina Elisabeta, Calea Victoriei, Str Știrbei Vodă and B-dul Schițu Măgureanu

Muzeul Național de Artă (National Art Museum)

The vast majority of this fine, neoclassical building ... 1812, when a rich merchant, Dinicu Golescu, had it built as a private home. His sons squandered their inheritance and sold it to the Romanian state in 1853. After Alexandru Ioan Cuza was elected to be first prince of the United Romanian Principalities in 1859, it became the Royal Palace, and was the main residence of all of Romania's kings: Carol I, Ferdinand, Carol II and Mihai. In 1944 the cabinet of wartime leader Ion Antonescu – who had sided with Germany – was arrested inside, marking Romania's withdrawal from the war. Since 1955 it has been the home of Romania's National Art Museum (see page 69).

ⓐ Piața Revoluției/Calea Victoriei 49–53 ☎ 021 313 30 30

Piața Amzei

A short walk north of the Athénée Palace, along Calea Victoriei, Str Piața Amzei leads you directly to the vibrant atmosphere of Piața Amzei, the city's busiest market. You can buy fresh fruit and vegetables, fish, meat, flowers and all kinds of household gadgets you never knew you needed. Or just sip coffee in a café and watch a lively and genuine street market at work.

Piața Revoluției

Piața Revoluției itself is today little more than a large open square of busy roads and car parks. On 21–22 December 1989, however, it was the scene of pitched battles between revolutionaries and security forces loyal to Ceaușescu. The bullet holes above the Humanitas bookshop on the south side are genuine, left as a memorial to the dead. A more obvious and far

⬤ *Piața Amzei: for all your fresh fruit and vegetable needs*

less moving memorial is the unsightly Revolution Monu
that sits in the middle of the square. Meant to signify freedom
breaking through barbed wire, locals say it looks more like an
olive on a cocktail stick. Look out for the brand new glass office
building (the headquarters of the Bucharest Architectural
Union) that has been built within the wrecked shell of a house
destroyed in the fighting.

Bulevardul Magheru & Piața Romana

Two minutes' walk west of Piața Amzei is Bulevardul Magheru,
all shops and banks, offices and hotels, and some of the city's
most expensive apartment blocks. The boulevard is busy night
and day, and the smell and noise of traffic are overwhelming at
rush hour. The boulevard's northern end tips out at Piața
Romana, more traffic junction than public square, but home to
the glorious and slightly dilapidated ASE, the economics faculty
of Bucharest University, built in 1929 to the designs of
Romanian architect Gregory Cerchez.

CULTURE

Biserica Crețulescu (Crețulescu Church)

The most famous church in the city, and one of the oldest, it was
built in 1720 by Iordache Crețulescu, a leading figure in the
Romanian cultural awakening of the 1700s. Damaged during
the fighting in 1989, it has been restored of late to exquisite
condition, and most of the original frescoes remain remarkably
intact. The finest are those on the doors, painted in 1858 by
Gheorghe Tattarescu. ❸ Calea Victoriei 47

● *Admire the art nouveau splendour of the George Enescu Museum*

Muzeul George Enescu (George Enescu Museum)

George Enescu was Romania's greatest composer, though he is perhaps better known in the Western world as a music teacher; he was the instructor of legendary violinist Yehudi Menuhin. The house was built for a merchant, George Cantacuzino, in the first decade of the 20th century, and betrays the French baroque preferences of its architect, Ion Berindei. It's worth visiting for the luxurious interiors of what is probably the finest private house ever built in Bucharest.

ⓐ Calea Victoriei 141 ☎ 021 659 63 65 🕐 10.00–17.00 Tues–Sun, closed Mon. Admission charge

Muzeul Național de Artă (National Art Museum)

There are three permanent exhibitions in this vast art museum, and all are worthy of your time. On the first floor you will find medieval Romanian art, featuring icons, altars and frescoes from any number of churches and monasteries, and one of Romania's oldest Bibles. The second floor shows modern Romanian art, with works by all of the Romanian 19th- and 20th-century greats, including painters Nicolae Grigorescu, Theodor Aman and Gheorghe Tattarescu. On the third floor is a small but decent collection of 20th-century European art.

ⓐ Calea Victoriei 49–53 ☎ 021 313 30 30 🕐 10.00–18.00 Wed–Sun, closed Mon & Tues. Admission charge

Sala Palatului

Behind (and attached via a walkway to) the National Art Museum is the Sala Palatului, famous among architects the world over for its unusual and gravity-defying concave roof.

Constructed in the 1950s, the building was used during the communist period to house the Romanian version of a parliament, the national assembly. It is today used for concerts, theatre productions and musicals. Check the box office on the ground floor for forthcoming attractions.

ⓐ Piața Palatului ⓛ Box office 10.00–19.00 Tues–Fri, closed Sat, Sun & Mon

RETAIL THERAPY

Casa del Havano Possibly the finest selection of genuine Cuban cigars in Europe. The knowledgeable and professional staff will help you choose the perfect cigar, or a gift from a wide range of smoking accessories. ⓐ Str Episcopiei 1–3 (Athénée Palace Hilton) ⓣ 021 311 15 81 ⓛ 10.00–23.00

Humanitas Besides books, the main interest for the visitor in this treasure trove will be the vast range of reproduction Orthodox religious icons, from conventional tempura on wood to more modern glass and naïve art icons. ⓐ Calea Victoriei 45 ⓣ 021 313 50 35 ⓦ www.librariilehumanitas.ro ⓛ 08.30–18.00 Mon–Fri, 09.00–14.00 Sat, closed Sun

Magazin Filatelic The official stamp shop of the Romanian Post Office. A wide range of antique and modern stamps, many portraying scenes from Romania's history. Communist-era stamps are usually the most sought after and expensive. ⓐ Str Ion Câmpineanu 27 ⓛ 09.30–18.00 Mon–Fri, 09.30–13.00 Sat, closed Sun

Piața Amzei The finest fresh fruit, vegetables and flowers that Romania has to offer. You can haggle if you know a little Romanian, but be warned: the old ladies behind the stalls know how to bargain. ⓐ Str Piața Amzei, near Piața Romană ⓛ 06.30–20.00 Mon–Fri, 06.30–18.00 Sat, 07.00–16.00 Sun

Romartizana A wide range of exquisite arts and crafts, all made by skilled Romanian craftsmen. Look out for the glass, lace, tablecloths and carved wooden figures. Mainstream souvenirs are here too, including dolls in national costume and Romanian flags. ⓐ Calea Victoriei 16–20 ⓣ 021 313 14 65 ⓦ www.romartizana.com.ro ⓔ romartizana@digicom.ro

TAKING A BREAK

Café & Terrace £ ❶ Few locations in the city top this, a terrace on Piața Revoluției. Good, cheap food and a wide range of coffee and exotic teas. Evenings are lively and in summer it's a popular outdoor nightlife spot, complete with DJs. ⓐ Str Franklin 12 ⓣ 021 310 10 17 ⓦ www.cafeterrace.ro ⓔ info@cafeterrace.ro ⓛ 12.00–02.00 Mon–Fri, 10.00–02.00 Sat & Sun

IO Expresso £ ❷ In the shell of a house destroyed during the revolution the Bucharest Architectural Union built their unique headquarters, and opened up the ground floor as a smart but reasonably priced café. ⓐ Str Demetri Dobrescu 5 ⓣ 021 315 60 98 ⓛ 09.00–24.00 Mon–Fri, 10.00–24.00 Sat & Sun

Caffe Frappe £–££ ❸   Huge windows make this the perfect spot to watch the bustle of Piața Amzei while sipping one of the city's better espressos. A little showy in high summer, and later in the evenings, when the 'in' crowd turns up. ⓐ Str Mendeleev 7–15, Piața Amzei ⓣ 021 212 90 84 ⓛ 09.00–24.00

La Strada ££ ❹   The best and most famous terrace in the city, perhaps even country, is this legend at the Athénée Palace. The food is great, the service exemplary and the prices are far cheaper than people expect. Barbecue nightly throughout the summer from 19.00. ⓐ Athénée Palace Hilton, Str Episcopiei 1–3 (access from Calea Victoriei) ⓣ 021 303 37 77 ⓛ 10.30–01.00 May–Sept

Studio £££ ❺   Trendy beyond words, this is one for the sunglasses crowd who seem to do little except stay here all day. Casual but wealthy visitors should stop by to see how Romania's rich set live. ⓐ Str C A Rosetti 10 ⓣ 021 315 72 98 ⓛ 08.00–01.00

Turabo £££ ❻   Serving cakes to die for, Turabo attracts a wide range of patrons, from students and backpackers to Romania's jet set. Despite the prices it's up there as the city's best café. ⓐ Str Episcopiei 6 ⓣ 0748 11 00 00 ⓦ www.turabo-cafe.ro ⓔ turabo-cafe@turabo-cafe.ro ⓛ 08.00–01.00

AFTER DARK

Restaurants
Bistro Ateneu £ ❼   This is how all Romanian restaurants should be: simple, delicious, cheap Romanian and Hungarian

food served by charming staff in gloriously fussy and scatty surroundings. No menu, the staff will bring you a blackboard with the day's offerings. ⓐ Str Episcopiei 3 ⓣ 021 313 49 00 ⓛ 12.00–01.00

Menuet £ ❽   Bargain food in a small, lively cellar setting behind Piața Revoluției. Food is Romanian with a French twist, and the wine list exemplary, featuring local and imported grapes. ⓐ Str Nicolae Golescu 14 ⓣ 021 312 01 43 ⓛ 12.30–00.30

Byblos ££ ❾   Next door to Menuet is this fantastic Italian restaurant, serving real trattoria food in an unfussy setting at prices that are worth paying, if not entirely cheap. Staff are friendly and the atmosphere clubby. It is great for larger groups. ⓐ Str Nicolae Golescu 14–16 ⓣ 021 313 20 91 ⓛ 12.00–24.00

La Mandragora ££ ❿   The German chef at this truly inventive modern European restaurant offers ever more daring combinations of ingredients, which seems to delight the increasingly knowledgeable Bucharest public. ⓐ Str Mendeleev 29 ⓣ 021 319 75 92 ⓛ 18.00–23.00

Balthazar £££ ⓫   Bucharest's best restaurant for almost five years, and still no real competition in sight. The food on an ever-changing and evolving fusion menu always includes new flavours. The wine list is a gem but, as with the food menu, everything on it costs a small fortune. ⓐ Str Dumbrava Rosie 2 ⓣ 021 212 14 60 ⓕ 021 212 14 61 ⓦ www.balthazar.ro ⓔ info@balthazar.ro ⓛ 12.00–24.00

Casa Vernescu £££ ⓬   A casino and restaurant where the French food is good, but it is the surroundings – a historic house on Bucharest's premier street – that people come for. ⓐ Calea Victoriei 133 ⓣ 021 311 97 44 ⓕ 021 311 16 45 ⓦ www.casavernescu.ro ⓔ office@casavernescu.ro ⓛ 18.30–01.00

Mazagran £££ ⓭   Decent fusion restaurant in the heart of Piața Amzei, with a great terrace that fills up very early in summer. If you want to sit outdoors, make a reservation. ⓐ Str Biserica Amzei 30 ⓣ 021 311 61 80 ⓛ 12.00–24.00, closed Mon

Roberto's £££ ⓮   The best Italian restaurant in the city. The menu – dedicated to one specific region of Italy at a time – changes every month. The Sicilian chef is indeed called Roberto. ⓐ Athénée Palace, Str Episcopiei 1–3 ⓣ 021 303 37 77 ⓕ 021 315 21 21 ⓛ 06.30–10.00, 12.00–15.00, 19.00–23.00 Mon–Fri, 06.30–11.00, 12.00–15.30, 19.00–23.00 Sat, 06.30–11.00, 19.00–23.00 Sun

Bars & clubs

Déjà vu The number one cocktail and good-time bar in Bucharest. If you do not particularly care about making a fool of yourself, get here. Ask for the 'extreme cocktails', which, with their audience participation, are more light cabaret than drinks. Great, loud music and a crowd that is refreshingly easy going. ⓐ B-dul Nicolae Bălcescu 25 ⓣ 021 311 23 22 ⓛ 12.00–04.00

English Bar Mellow and historic, this is the only bar in the city to have a leading role in a novel: Olivia Manning's *Balkan Trilogy*.

Comfy leather seats and friendly staff await, as do the expat regulars who swear by the place. ⓐ Athénée Palace Hilton, Str Episcopiei 1–3 ☎ 021 303 37 77 ext 3962 ⏰ 11.00–02.00

The Office Established in 1998 and still the best club in the city centre. Expect an eclectic mix of music, a wealthy but not extravagant crowd, a great range of imported wine and champagne, and the best dancers in Bucharest. Dress well if you want to get in. ⓐ Str Tache Ionescu 2 ☎ 021 211 67 48 & 0745 11 00 64 ⓦ www.theoffice.ro ⏰ 21.30–05.00 Fri & Sat, 22.00–02.00 Sun, closed Mon–Thur

Arts venues

Ateneu Român This stunning concert hall was built in 1888, and has hosted the city's finest orchestras ever since. It today plays host to the George Enescu Philharmonic, which performs classical concerts most evenings. The best and most popular concerts take place on Fridays, when booking in advance is a must. ⓐ Str Franklin 1 ☎ 021 315 25 67 ⓦ www.bucharest-philharmonic.ro ⏰ Box office 10.00–12.00, 16.00–18.30 Mon–Fri, 10.00–12.00 Sat & Sun

Green Hours 22 Jazz Café Jazz, and good jazz at that. There are concerts most nights of the week in a gorgeous little venue in a courtyard off Calea Victoriei. You need to make reservations for the more popular concerts at weekends. Mondays have recently been given over to experimental theatre, and there are often art exhibitions here too. ⓐ Calea Victoriei 120 ☎ 021 314 57 51 ☏ 021 211 95 92 ⓦ www.green-hours.ro ⏰ 24 hrs

Universitate, Lipscani & Unirii

Piața Universității (known as Universitate) is a city centre
waiting to happen. At the moment, however, it remains a
phenomenally busy junction, and crossing it involves using the
rather grotty metro underpass. Nevertheless, it is the gateway
to the most interesting parts of the city, and its main landmark,
the InterContinental hotel, is a good beacon if you get lost.
The National Theatre is here too, and the city's most picture-
postcard church stands on the square's fringes. Piața Unirii is
the result of decades of central planning, a vast expanse of
concrete designed for the new socialist man Nicolae Ceaușescu
claimed to be attempting to create. Linking Universitate and
Unirii is the quirky, eccentric and rough-around-the-edges
Lipscani district, all that is left of old Bucharest.

SIGHTS & ATTRACTIONS

Biserica Studenților Sf Nicolae (St Nicholas (Russian) Church)
Built with donations of gold roubles from Russian Tsar Nicholas
II in 1904–9, this church – always referred to as the Russian
Church – is famous for its onion domes and gold leaf trimmings.
ⓐ Str Ion Ghica 9

Casa Poporului (House of the People)
Romania's best-known landmark is the infamous Casa
Poporului. It was designed to be the crowning achievement in
the life and career of Nicolae Ceaușescu, who demolished
countless thousands of houses, tens of churches, a stadium,

a monastery and two hospitals to make way for it.
Construction began in 1984, and at the time of the dictator's
death in 1989 it was all but completed. It is reputedly the
second-largest building in the world (after the Pentagon). It is
certainly big; the building is almost 100 m (328 ft) high and
more than 3 km (2 miles) in circumference. It today hosts
the Romanian Parliament, the Senate and the Museum of
Contemporary Art.

⊘ Calea 13 Septembrie 1, entrance A3 ❶ 021 311 36 11
🕐 10.00–16.00. Admission charge

Curtea Veche (Old Court Church & Palace)

Bucharest first became an important city when Vlad III Țepeș
moved his court here in the 1450s and built a princely palace.
Little of the palace remains, most of it having been destroyed by
a series of fires in the 19th century. The remains we see today
were in fact only uncovered in 1967 during archaeological digs
at the site. The exquisitely preserved church next door is the
oldest in the city (1545). ⊘ Str Franceză

🔺 *The Casa Poporului is one of the city's most popular attractions*

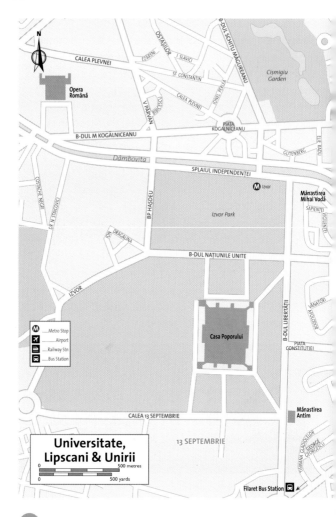

Universitate,
Lipscani & Unirii

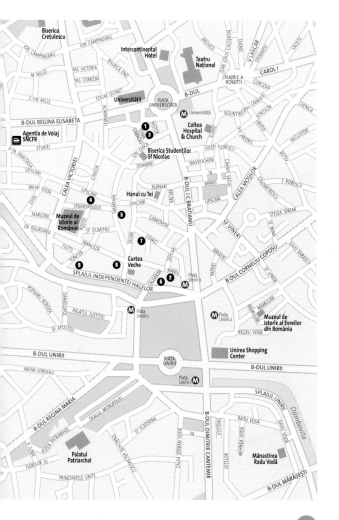

Hanul cu Tei

Han in Romanian means *inn*, and Bucharest was once full of
places like this, where traders and travellers could rest their
horses in the stables, enjoy a drink and a meal and even stay the
night. The Hanul cu Tei (Inn Under the Trees) is today one of the
few that remain intact, though its original purpose has long
changed. Instead of highwaymen and their horses, you will
instead find the best selection of art and craft workshops and
outlets in Bucharest (see page 85). ❸ Str Lipscani 63–65
🕓 09.00–18.00 Mon–Fri, 09.00–14.00 Sat & Sun

Lipscani

Strada Lipscani is actually one street that runs through the
heart of Old Bucharest, but it has lent its name to the whole
historic area. According to legend, traders from Leipzig pitched
here one day in the 17th century and left their name, Leipzig
becoming, over the years, Lipscani. Today the area is all that
survives of the old city, which grew up around the princely court
which Vlad III Țepeș moved here in the 15th century.

Much of the dilapidated but clearly glorious architecture of
its houses – many built for rich merchants in secession style at
the turn of the 20th century, when the area first became really
fashionable – gives an idea as to how the whole city must have
once looked. It is a great area to explore, and surprises lurk at
every corner, from the enormous neoclassical National Bank at
Strada Lipscani 25 to the remains of the old princely court itself
on Strada Franceza.

Mănastirea Mihai Vodă (Mihai Vodă Monastery)

This neo-Byzantine-style monastery, which dates from 1601, was moved – on rails – 285 m (935 ft) west in 1985 to make way for the apartment blocks that now hide it from view. It suffered structural damage as a result, and its interior frescoes were badly cracked. Restoration continues and the place occasionally closes without warning. ⓐ Str Sapienței 2

Mănastirea Radu Vodă (Radu Vodă Monastery)

Though well hidden behind Piața Unirii's apartment blocks, it is worth hunting this monastery down, if only for the tranquillity of its gardens and grounds. The monastery church dates from 1613 and is a smaller copy of the Curtea de Argeș at Pitești. It was extensively rebuilt and restored in the 19th century, when Gheorghe Tattarescu added the divine frescoes.
ⓐ Str Radu Vodă 24A

Palatul Patriarchal (Patriarchal Palace)

This building has been the spiritual heart of the Romanian Orthodox Church since it was first built in the late 17th century (most of the current complex dates from the early 20th century). It remains the home of the head of the church, Patriarch Teoctist, and its gorgeous little church is open only for services (daily at around 11.00 and 17.00) and on certain saints' days. You can, however, freely admire the exterior and the sublime bell tower (from 1698) at the entrance to the complex.
ⓐ Str Dealul Mitropoliei

Piața Universității

For history fans Piața Universității is the most important place in Bucharest. Though Romania's revolution began elsewhere (at Piața Revoluției), it was here that the back of the communist regime was broken, on the night of 21–22 December 1989. In the traffic island in the middle of the square crosses commemorate those who died here, including Mihai Gatlan, Bucharest's first revolutionary victim, who was killed at 17.30 on 21 December. The square was also the scene of the Mineriada (Miners' Riot) of June 1990, when miners from the Jiu Valley were brought in by then President Ion Iliescu to put down a student protest against his regime. More than 100 were killed over two days. More recently the square has been the scene of happier events; it is where the city's residents come to celebrate important victories in sport, stopping traffic as they do so.

Besides the InterContinental and the National Theatre, the square's other landmark is the eponymous University (Universitatea). The main building (whose neoclassical façade is actually on Bulevardul Regina Elisabeta) was constructed in 1857, and boasts sublime bas-reliefs on the upper levels of its central section.

Piața & Bulevardul Unirii

No post-war city in Europe changed as much as southern Bucharest did from 1984 to 1989. It is a chilling experience to compare a map of Bucharest from the early 1980s with one from today. The longest, widest street in the city, Bulevardul Unirii, did not exist, neither did most of Piața Unirii, Calea 13 September or Bulevardul Libertatii, the streets which run in front of and alongside the Casa Poporului. Instead, a maze of narrow streets lined with charming *fin-de-siècle* houses filled the space. The entire district was razed in 1984 to make way for a new Civic Centre, the design of which was allegedly based on that of the North Korean capital, Pyongyang.

The idea of building the Civic Centre, with the Casa Poporului as its central point, was to create a city within a city, one in which all of the organs of the communist state could be housed, along with the functionaries needed to run them.

◯ *The glorious interior of the Radu Vodă Monastery church*

THE CITY

The apartments that line Bulevardul Unirii were not built for the people whose houses were knocked down to make way for them; they were instead given tiny, unheated apartments in the far northwest of Bucharest. Only the very cream of communist society was to live in the Civic Centre, in isolation from the miserable souls whose lives they ruined.

CULTURE

Muzeul de Istorie al Evreilor din România (Jewish History Museum)

Housed in a former synagogue dating from 1850, this museum tells the story of Romania's once large Jewish community (which numbered 700,000 before World War II) as well as outlining the horrific events that culminated in the murder of more than half of them during the Holocaust. Bucharest's Jewish population now totals just 4,000.

ⓐ Str Mamulari 3 ❶ 021 311 08 70 🕓 09.00–13.00 Mon–Wed, Fri & Sun, 09.00–16.00 Thur, closed Sat

Muzeul de Istorie al României (National History Museum)

Romania's National History Museum is housed inside a wonderful neoclassical building constructed in 1894–6, originally used as the headquarters of the Romanian Post Office. Its finest exhibitions are downstairs in the Lapidarium, and include a full-scale replica of Trajan's Column.

ⓐ Calea Victoriei 12 ❶ 021 315 82 07 ❶ 021 311 33 56
🅦 www.mnir.ro 🕓 10.00–18.00 Tues–Sun, closed Mon. Admission charge

Teatru Național (National Theatre)

This is in fact two buildings in one. The original National Theatre was built in 1967–70 and was styled as a modernist tribute to the steep-roofed wooden churches of the Maramureș, a region in the far north of Romania. When Elena Ceaușescu became directly responsible for the Ministry of Culture in the late 1970s, however, she ordered the building covered with the (not unappealing) neoclassical casing we see today. Inside the main lobby you can see how the newer structure was placed over the old.

ⓐ Piața 21 Decembrie 1989

RETAIL THERAPY

Hanul cu Tei This is a collective of artisans who all exhibit their wares in the courtyard of a former inn. There are a dozen shops in all, and you can find lace, porcelain, pottery and paintings.

ⓐ Str Lipscani 63–65 ☎ 021 315 56 63 🅕 021 315 03 27
🕐 10.00–18.00 Mon–Fri, 10.00–14.00 Sat & Sun

Sticerom Like Hanul cu Tei, this is a collective of artisans. Look out for high-quality glass (made on the premises), including richly colourful glass icons.

ⓐ Str Selari 9–11 ☎ 021 314 94 92 🅕 021 314 67 65
🕐 09.30–18.00 Mon–Fri, 09.30–15.00 Sat, closed Sun

Unirea Hundreds of small concessions sell everything imaginable from perfumes to fashion, hi-tech gadgets to hi-fis.

ⓐ Piața Unirii 1 ☎ 021 303 03 07 🅦 www.unireashop.ro
🕐 09.00–22.00 Mon–Sat, 09.00–18.00 Sun

TAKING A BREAK

Alsy £ ❶ This is the most central café in town, with its terrace offering a prize view of Piața Universității in summer. In winter the tiny interior becomes a very smoky place. ⓐ Str Toma Caragiu 3 ☎ 0721 40 82 36 🕐 08.00–01.00

Hanul lui Manuc £ ❷ The last remaining *Han* in Bucharest that has retained its original features, this place offers cheap beer,

🔺 *Making the most of the summer terrace at Cremcaffé*

cheap Romanian food and beds for the night. ⓐ Str Franceză 62–64 ⓣ 021 313 14 15 ⓕ 021 312 28 11 ⓛ 10.00–23.00

Cremcaffé ££ ❸ With an apple pie that brings in clients from all over the city, Cremcaffé is always full. ⓐ Str Toma Caragiu 3 ⓣ 021 313 97 40 ⓕ 021 313 97 48 ⓛ 07.30–24.00 Mon–Fri, 09.00–24.00 Sat & Sun

Market 8 ££ ❹ Café, shop, art gallery… just the kind of trendy place that is currently giving the Lipscani district such a good name. ⓐ Str Stavropoleos 8 ⓣ 021 313 41 67 ⓛ 10.00–21.30 Mon–Sat, closed Sun

Charme £££ ❺ The most classy and expensive of the new Lipscani cafés, frequented by a somewhat affected crowd. Sexy velvet sofas and great sandwiches. ⓐ Str Smardan 12 ⓛ 11.30–01.00

Festival 39 £££ ❻ Serving coffee and simple food. The tables by the windows – which look out onto Piaţa Unirii – are top see-and-be-seen spots. ⓐ Str Franceză 64 (entrance on Piaţa Unirii) ⓛ 11.00–01.00 Mon–Fri, 15.00–24.00 Sun

AFTER DARK

Restaurants
Amsterdam £ ❼ By day a lunch and meeting venue, serving great goulash among other things, by night a lively bar, with a disco downstairs. ⓐ Str Covaci 6 ⓣ 021 313 75 81 ⓕ 021 313 75 80 ⓦ www.amsterdam.ro ⓔ info@amsterdam.ro ⓛ 10.00–01.00

St George £ ❶ Bucharest's best Hungarian restaurant. Enjoy fine fresh goose liver and *Debrecener* sausages in a lively dining room setting before washing it all down with one of the five Azsu dessert wines. ⓐ Str Franceză 44 ❶ 021 317 10 87 Ⓦ www.stgeorge.ro ❶ 09.00–23.00

Count Dracula ££ ❷ Good Romanian food given a lively twist by the chap dressed as Dracula who pops out of a coffin and does a tour of the tables at some stage during the evening. ⓐ Spl Independenţei 8A ❶ 021 312 13 53 Ⓦ www.count-dracula.ro ❶ 15.00–01.00, closed Sun

Bars & clubs

Club A The students' favourite. Cheap drinks, music from all genres and all eras, and a no-hassle atmosphere make this just about the best thing to do in Bucharest of a night. ⓐ Str Blanari 14 ❶ 021 313 55 92 ❶ 10.00–05.00 Mon–Fri, 21.00–06.00 Sat & Sun

Exit Downstairs at Amsterdam is this superb nightclub, where DJs play the latest tunes on Friday and Saturday nights. The cocktail list runs to several pages. ⓐ Str Covaci 6 ❶ 021 313 75 80 Ⓦ www.amsterdam.ro ⓔ exit@amsterdam.ro ❶ 21.00–04.00 Fri & Sat, closed Mon–Thur & Sun

Harp An Irish pub as good as they come. Great-value Irish and British food, such as shepherd's pie, and an oasis of decent service. It can get lively in the evenings. ⓐ Str Bibescu Vodă 1 ❶ 021 335 65 08 ❶ 09.00–02.00 ❶ reservations are essential at weekends

Temple The all-female bar staff are half the attraction for some, while the good mainstream music and friendly crowd make it a good choice for anyone. It's not cheap though. ⓐ Splaiul Independenței, corner of Str Selari ⓣ 0727 29 76 10
ⓛ 17.00–05.00 Mon–Wed, 22.00–05.00 Thur–Sat, closed Sun & Mon

Whispers Serving the best English breakfast in Bucharest, this pub and grill is a favourite with the expat community that throngs here to watch English football, cricket and rugby on the large screens. ⓐ Str Ion Brezoianu 4 ⓣ 021 314 29 01
ⓛ 09.00–01.00 Mon–Fri, 12.00–01.00 Sat & Sun

Arts venues

Opera Română The Romanian National Opera sticks to a simple and well-known repertoire. While a lack of funding means sets are less than spectacular, the standard of performers is high. All performances except Sunday matinees begin at 18.30.
ⓐ B-dul Mihail Kogălniceanu 70–72 ⓣ 021 314 69 80
ⓦ www.operanb.ro ⓛ Box office 10.00–12.00

Teatru Național There is unlikely to be that much on at the National Theatre to interest non-Romanian speakers, though sometimes the venue is used for major concerts and shows. Check listings for details. ⓐ Piața 21 Decembrie 1989
ⓣ 021 314 71 71 ⓛ Box office 10.00–16.00 Mon, 10.00–18.00 Tues–Sun

Northern Bucharest

The leafy northern part of Bucharest is where the city's rich or
well-connected live, and where the whole city comes to play, in
Herăstrău, the largest park in the city. Characterised by wide
boulevards and set-piece buildings, some of the distances
between sights in this part of Bucharest are long, and you may
be jumping in and out of taxis some of the time. Fortunately,
however, many of the sights in northern Bucharest are half or
even a full day's outing in themselves, including the Village
Museum, Peasant Museum and Herăstrău Park.

SIGHTS & ATTRACTIONS

Arc de Triumf
It is likely that you will see the Arc de Triumf for the first time as
you drive in from the airport. Slightly smaller than its more
famous namesake in Paris, the Arc was built in 1930 to honour
those killed in World War I; it replaced a 1919 wooden structure.
The viewing gallery at the top is currently closed to the public.
ⓐ Piața Arcul de Triumf

Casa Scanteii/Casa Presei Libere
At the head of Șos Kiseleff, this monolithic building is often
mistaken by first-time visitors for the Casa Poporului. This is an
earlier construction, the first major socialist building project to
be completed (in 1956, mainly by forced labourers), and is a
smaller replica of the Palace of Science and Culture in Warsaw,
Poland. Designed by local architect Horia Maicu it was built to

house all of the communist-era newspapers, as well as the state press agency. It still serves much the same purpose, though the newspapers inside are all now in private hands. You can wander in to admit the marble entrance hall, but nothing else.

ⓐ Piața Presei Libere 1

Herăstrău Park

Set over 187 hectares (462 acres) this wonderful park is where much of the city comes to spend warm weekend afternoons. It

🔺 *The Arc de Triumf commemorates Romania's Great War dead*

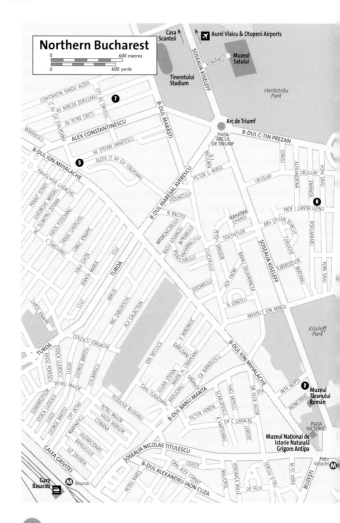

Northern Bucharest

0 ————————— 600 metres
0 ————————— 600 yards

Casa Scanteii

Aurel Vlaicu & Otopeni Airports

Muzeul Satului

Tineretului Stadium

Herăstrău Park

Arc de Triumf

CONSTANTIN SANDU ALDEA

LT AV CH STALPEANU

AV MIRCEA ZORILEANU

AV PETRE CRETU

AL DROSU

7

B-DUL MARASTI

ROMÂNEŞTI

SOSEAUA KISELEFF

PIATA ARCUL DE TRIUMF

B-DUL C-TIN PREZAN

MARASESCU

ALEX CONSTANTINESCU

AV STEFAN SANATESCU

ALEEA LT AV CH STALPEANU

5

B-DUL ION MIHALACHE

PARASCHIVA GHERGHEL

GHEORGE MISGAL

ING DIMITRU TOMA

VIRGIL PLESOIANU

VASILE CIRICOREL

C BURICEANU

CARG KNAPPE

HAG GHITA

SFANTA MARIA

CLUJ

TURDA

ABRUD

ING ZABLOVSCHI

ALA GALACTION

V LY DRN

PICTOR G MIREA

STOLNICULUI

N RACOTA

MORENCHOLOS

RADU BOSANGU

PITON CICERULUI

SF BASILIUS

PAHARNICULUI

CUCERPULUI

CISCIFILOLUI

ADV ENORE

SERDARULUI

ARH STEFAN FURICUS

MAHATMA GHANDI

DOCENTILOR

PETRU SANDOR

BARBU DELAVRANCEA

N IONESCU

ARHITECT ION MINCU

SOSEAUA KISELEFF

CRISOFER

POPA SAVU

EMANOIL

URUGUAY

ALEXANDRINA

SORIN

URUGUAY

PROF I CANTACUZINO

POPULAREANU

TUBEROZELOR

BRATIANU

POPA SAVU

Kiseleff Park

TURDA

CAROL FNATNO

RADU POPESCU

STOICA LUDESCU

GEORGE BARITIU

GOLESCU IORDACHE

COCIARESCU

ION NICULESCU

V MIRONESC

OARCEANU

MATA AL CAMPEANU

B-DUL ION MIHALACHE

INTR NOPTII

2 Muzeul Țăranului Român

MIONETESTI

DR LITLA

DR FELIX IACOB

PETRU MAJOR

SOMMERSTOR

STOICA LUDESCU

LUGOJ

CPT OCTN

GEORGE BARITIU

PETRU MAJOR

TEODOSIE RUDEANU

VALEA MORILOR

PICTOR HENTIA

SCARLETESCU

A VARTEANU

DR C CARACAS

DR FELIX IACOB

LIEBERT

PIATA VICTORIEI

C MARINESCU

JACOMICOARE

BAHLUIULUI

SILT ZAHARIA

GRAL VLADOIANU

RADICANU

MASOR E MANOLESCU

HAG MOSOC

SOSEAUA NICOLAE TITULESCU

Muzeul National de Istorie Naturală Grigore Antipa

CALEA GRIVITEI

SOSEAUA NICOLAE TITULESCU

B-DUL ALEXANDRU IAON CUZA

GRAL ALEX CERNAT

COIESTI

VERONICA MICLE

MALDDOL

M-TII ATEA

SERGIU DO FRUL

BUZESTI

PIATA Victoriei **M**

Gara Basarab **M** Basarab

PETRI RARES

DR FELIX

GENERAL

MANTA

B-DUL BANU MANTA

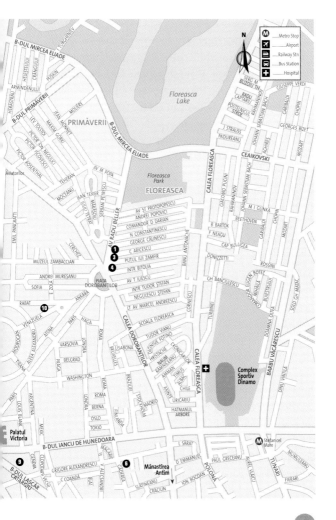

sits around a vast lake and much of it has recently been restored to pristine condition. It boasts a number of alleys and paths, all lined with a wide variety of native Romanian flowers, as well as numerous spots for picnic lunches. There are pleasure-boat rides around the lake during the summer, and a couple of launches for sailing boats which can be hired. For the less nautically experienced, pedalo boats are popular. On the northern shore is a raft of terraces, a go-cart track and a small amusement park with old-fashioned roller coasters, dodgems and trampolines. The main entrance is from Piața Charles de Gaulle, which was recently decorated with a large bronze statue of the great French general.
🅐 Șos Kiseleff/Piața Charles de Gaulle

Piața Victoriei
Only slightly smaller than Piața Unirii, Piața Victoriei is another of Bucharest's squares ruined by traffic. Its saving grace is the sleek government building on the eastern side, with a neoclassical façade and originally the home of the Foreign Ministry. The southern side is all communist blocks, while the northern is home to Bucharest's tallest skyscraper, the 120-m (394-ft) Europa House (the HQ of a bank and closed to the public). The square is completed by three museums: the Grigore Antipa Museum of Natural History, a stunning place both inside and out; the National Peasant Museum, the city's finest; and the Geology Museum, a dull collection of rocks.

Șoseaua Kiseleff
Named after a popular Russian general who did much for the city during his station here in the mid-19th century, Kiseleff

(Kiselev on older maps) is Bucharest's Park Lane. Gorgeous villas stand in detached isolation and sumptuous grounds. Most are too big to run as private residences, and many have been converted into banking headquarters, foreign embassies or car showrooms. A walk along this street is a stark reminder of how rich the Bucharest bourgeoisie once was, and a great introduction to the idiosyncrasies of Romanian architecture. The small park at the southern end has a good children's playground.

CULTURE

Mănastirea Antim (Antim Monastery)

The patriarch of the Orthodox Church, Antim Ivreanul, had this monastery built in 1708 and gave it his name. It is topped by a stunning gold-plated dome, and its church is fronted by carved wooden doors, the work of Ivreanul himself. Inside there are frescoes from 1812 depicting the Nativity and some gruesome scenes from Revelations.

ⓐ Str Antim 29

Muzeul Național de Istorie Naturală Grigore Antipa (Grigore Antipa Museum of Natural History)

The recently renovated exterior of this cracking museum is as much an attraction as the exhibitions inside. There are displays of fossils and long-extinct animals, including a woolly mammoth, as well as the only complete dinosaur skeleton in the country. In the basement there is a fantastic display of sea life, and everything is brilliantly presented with Romanian and

English captions. There is also an ever-increasing number of interactive displays, and it is a great place to bring children. Beware though; there is also a display of live reptiles complete with lizards, snakes and baby alligators.

ⓐ Șos Kiseleff 1 ⓣ 021 312 88 26 ⓕ 021 312 88 63
ⓦ www.antipa.ro ⓛ 10.00–19.00 Wed–Sun, closed Mon & Tues. Admission charge

⬥ *The Antim Monastery church – don't miss the carvings on the doors*

Muzeul Satului (Village Museum)

King Carol II founded this open-air museum in 1936 so that
Bucharest's urbanites could see how the peasantry lived. He had
more than 60 houses, farmsteads, stables, windmills, watermills
and even a church brought here from all of Romania's regions.
Every exhibit is well labelled, many with recordings (in English
and Romanian) explaining the history of the house and its
region. Most people flock first to the extraordinary church of the
Maramureș, an enormous wooden building from the early 18th
century, whose faded but visible frescoes whet the appetite for
a visit to the remote Maramureș region itself, where every
village has at least one such church. The museum has a great
gift shop, and a stall outside sells Romanian sweet delicacies.
ⓐ Șos Kiseleff 28–30 ⓣ 021 222 91 06 ⓕ 021 222 90 68
ⓦ www.muzeul-satului.ro ⓛ 09.00–19.00 Tues–Sun,
10.00–17.00 Mon ⓘ Open all year round but some houses and
buildings close during winter. Admission charge

Muzeul Țăranului Român (Peasant Museum)

Bucharest's best museum. You can spend the best part of a day
trawling around the thousands upon thousands of exhibits that
display the ingenuity, craft and skill of the Romanian peasant.
Enjoy vivid descriptions of country life, traditions and the
histories of the particular group of Romanians who executed
the work. Most popular are the intricately painted Easter eggs
Romanians used to give each other at Easter (but now seldom
do); you can buy replicas in the superb gift shop. Look out, too,
for the religious art, from carved icons to sacred texts woven
into fabric, as well as the vast room presenting traditional

costumes from Romania's regions. In the basement is an exhibition of communism, a vast collection of portraits, busts, flags, banners, emblems and newspaper articles from the darkest era of Romania's recent past. It is the only place in the city you will still find a portrait of Nicolae Ceaușescu.

ⓐ Șos Kiseleff 3 ❶ 021 650 53 60 🕐 10.00–18.00 Tues–Sun, closed Mon. Admission charge

RETAIL THERAPY

Mario Plaza In wealthy Dorobanti this exclusive shopping mall is the well-located home to a small number of high-end fashion

🔺 *Head to the Peasant Museum for authentic Romanian souvenirs*

shops for men, women and children, perfumeries, interior design outlets, a good bookshop and a trendy café. ⓐ Calea Dorobanţilor 172 ⓣ 021 230 47 71 ⓕ 021 230 41 20 ⓦ www.marioplaza.ro ⓛ 10.00–21.00 Mon–Sat, 10.00–14.00 Sun

Peasant Museum If you do not find a souvenir at this place then you are really in trouble. If it is made in Romania and it involves skill and craft you will find it, from full national costume to charming wooden carved figures. Prices are not cheap but everyone will find something they can afford. ⓐ Şos Kiseleff 3 ⓣ 021 650 53 60

Village Museum A smaller version of the Peasant Museum shop, with more of an emphasis placed on religious objects, icons and books. ⓐ Şos Kiseleff 28–30 ⓣ 021 222 91 06 ⓕ 021 222 90 68 ⓦ www.muzeul-satului.ro

TAKING A BREAK

When it comes to cafés, one street in Bucharest is head and shoulders above all others: Strada Radu Beller, where it meets Piaţa Dorobanţilor. It is lined with coffee houses and is the closest thing Bucharest gets to a 'strip'.

La Belle Epoque ££ ❶ A Belgian beer café with only the finest Belgian beers, from conventional Stella Artois and Hoegaarden to less well-known Trappist beers such as Chimay. The good food menu is well priced. ⓐ Str Radu Beller 6 ⓣ 021 230 07 70 ⓛ 11.30–24.00

Casa Doina ££ ❷ This is one of the oldest restaurants in the city, designed for the Romanian Pavilion at the 1904 World Fair. It didn't make the fair, so was instead erected in the heart of Bucharest's smartest suburb. Great Romanian and international dishes. During the day it is a charming place for a good-value lunch. ⓐ Șos Kiseleff 4 ❶ 021 222 31 79 🖶 021 222 67 18 ⓦ www.casadoina.ro 🕒 11.00–01.00

Saga ££ ❸ This is the newest of the Radu Beller coffee houses, and, my, how good it is. The windows are huge and set right up against the street, making it the perfect place to see and be seen. The coffee is great and there is a good selection of cakes and snacks. ⓐ Str Radu Beller 6 ❶ 021 231 55 40 🕒 08.00–23.00 Mon–Thur, 08.00–24.00 Fri–Sat, 09.00–23.00 Sun

High Heels £££ ❹ This place has not just coffee, cakes and style, but shoes, sold in the adjacent showroom. Now ladies who lunch can buy a pair of unique, locally designed shoes while sipping espressos. Who said Romania was not ready for the EU? ⓐ Str Radu Beller 4 ❶ 021 230 70 40 🕒 08.00–01.00

AFTER DARK

Restaurants
Barka Saffron £–££ ❺ Something of a legend, this place has the best staff, the liveliest atmosphere and the coolest owner in town. Great cocktails, a mix of Indian and Indonesian food, great tapas, good sounds and parties galore. ⓐ Str Av Sănătescu 1 ❶ 021 224 10 04 🕒 12.00–23.30 Mon–Fri, 10.00–23.30 Sat & Sun

La Bastille ££ ❻ Charming French restaurant where food is treated as art and the staff are efficient and knowledgeable. Prices are remarkably good. Try to get a table in the upstairs dining room. ⓐ Str Căderea Bastiliei 72B ❶ 021 310 73 59 ❶ 021 310 73 60 ⓦ www.labastille.ro ❶ 12.00–24.00

Thai Moods ££ ❼ Authentic, tasty Thai food. Best during the summer, when the big garden out back is open. At other times make a reservation, as there are just a few tables inside. ⓐ Str Petre Crețu 63 ❶ 021 224 68 51 or 0723 17 40 39 ⓦ www.thaimoods.ro ❶ 12.00–24.00, closed Mon

Arcade £££ ❽ A luxurious place with fine food. The vaguely Italian menu has some modern European touches. ⓐ Str I Cantacuzino 8 ❶ 021 260 29 60 ❶ 12.00–24.00

Casa di David Downtown £££ ❾ Probably the best place in the city for quality fish and seafood. It's expensive, but worth every penny. ⓐ Str Lascar Catargiu 56 ❶ 021 317 45 51 ❶ 12.00–24.00

Uptown £££ ❿ What brings people to this place is the terrace, covered by a heated canopy that means you can sit outside in December. The food is inventive if a little overpriced, but the home-made butter is the best around. ⓐ Str Rabat 2 ❶ 021 231 40 77 ❶ 021 230 13 60 ❶ 10.00–24.00

Bars & clubs

Bamboo A flashy nightspot on Lake Tei. It is best in summer when the trendy crowd spills out onto the terrace. Expect a

more mainstream disco soundtrack than elsewhere. ⓐ Str
Rămuri Tei 39 ⓣ 0788 29 67 76 ⓦ www.bamboosportingclub.ro
🕓 23.30–06.00 Thur–Sat, closed Mon–Wed & Sun

Dubliner The original expat pub, the Dubliner offers live British
sports, steak and kidney pie, the city's best jukebox and a
covered terrace which is great in winter. ⓐ B-dul N Titulescu 18
ⓣ 021 222 94 73 ⓦ www.irishpubs.ro 🕓 09.00–02.00

Kristal Glam Club Kristal almost single-handedly turned the
Romanian capital into a decent club venue. Expect the best local
and international DJs and expensive drinks. Sitting at a table
costs €100, so come prepared to dance. ⓐ Str J S Bach 2
ⓣ 021 231 21 36 ⓦ www.clubkristal.ro 🕓 22.00–05.00 Thur–Sun,
closed Mon–Wed

Studio Martin Expect only the biggest names in club music
from around the world. Entrance ticket costs vary with the stock
value of the DJ in question. ⓐ B-dul Iancu de Hunedoara 41
ⓦ www.themission.ro 🕓 22.00–05.00 Fri & Sat, closed
Mon–Thur & Sun

White Horse Lively pub and restaurant in the Dorobanti area of
the city. Popular with locals and expats, it can get very lively on
weekend evenings. ⓐ Str George Călinescu 4A ⓣ 021 231 27 95
🕓 12.30–24.00

▶ *The stunning Transylvanian Alps, north of Bucharest*

OUT OF TOWN
trips

Around Bucharest: lakes, palaces & monasteries

Bucharest stands somewhat isolated on the plain of Wallachia, surrounded in the main by small villages with no interest for the visitor. There are some worthwhile excursions, however, mainly the medieval monasteries built to give thanks for victory in battle, and the 18th-century palaces that were built to house the city's rich in splendid isolation. There are also lakes and forests, nature reserves and Eastern Europe's largest film studio.

GETTING THERE

There are trains from Gara de Nord during summer weekends to Mogoșoaia and Snagov, though they are of the dirty, slow type and are not recommended. The stations are also some distance from the attractions they serve. It is a better idea to take the buses: no. 444 from Piața Presei Libere for Snagov, and no. 460 from Laromet for Mogoșoaia and Buftea. There is no public transport to Caldarușani. Bucharest taxis will bring you out to all of the places featured here, though note that tariffs double once you leave the city limits, and rare is the taxi driver who will drive out here to bring you home at the end of the day. Indeed, the only way to see all of these sights and attractions is with your own car (see details of car hire on page 58). It takes around 30 minutes by car to get to all of these places, double that by public transport.

SIGHTS & ATTRACTIONS

Lacul Snagov (Snagov Lake)

The largest of the lakes which surround Bucharest, Snagov,
37 km (23 miles) north of the city, has a long history as a summer
recreational retreat for Bucharest's block-bound residents. More
recently it has become their home; more than 1,200 villas now
surround all sides of the lake. Many people still come here for the
day, however, to fish, barbecue, swim in the lake, hire rowing
boats or cycle in the surrounding forests. For the active visitor, a
day here can be rewarding. You can paddle kayaks (with or
without an instructor), take a speedboat ride, play tennis or even
learn how to scuba dive. All of these activities take place at
Snagov Beach (Snagov Plaja) on the southern side of the lake.
Speedboat trips have to be arranged in advance with Snagov Tur
in Bucharest (❶ (021) 322 59 87). South of the lake is a small
nature reserve, Snagov Rezervat, whose flora and fauna, including
deer, stags, pheasants and owls, are protected. A number of bird-
watching posts have been set up around the reserve.
ⓐ Complex Turistic Snagov, Sat Snagov, Comuna Snagov
❶ (021) 323 99 25

Mănastirea Caldaruşani (Caldaruşani Monastery)

Situated on a peninsula 6 km (3¹/₂ miles) southeast of Snagov
Lake, the monastery of Caldaruşani was built in 1637 by Matei
Basarab, then ruler of Wallachia, to give thanks for victory over
Moldavian Prince Vasile Lupu in the Battle of Teleajen. The
structure of the three-towered monastery church remains, but
the frescoes inside have faded badly, though those featuring

Bucharest region

0 _____ 50 km
0 _____ 25 miles

Sibiu
Făgăraș
Rupea
Târgu Secuiesc
Soveja
Sfântu Gheorghe
Avrig
Hârtibaciu
Olt
Putna
Codlea
Brașov
Întorsura Burzăului
Zăbala
Vârful Suru 2283
Vârful Moldoveanu 2544
Munții Piatra Craiului
Râșnov
Vârful Ciucaș 1954
Buzău
Nehoiu
Bâsca Mică
Transylvanian Alps
Rucăr
Munții Bucegi
Castelul Peleș
Sinaia
Vălenii de Munte
Dealul Istrița 749
Călimănești
Curtea de Argeș
Bolboci Lake
Câmpina
Râmnicu Vâlcea
Colibași
Pucioasa
Băico
Mizil
Târgoviște
Ploiești
Urziceni
Pitești
Prahova
Drăgășani
Costești
Găești
Titu
Otopeni International Airport
Lacul Snagov
Mânăstirea Caldarușani
Scornicești
Teleorman
Bâftea
Mogoșoaia
A1
Aurel Vlaicu International Airport
Fundulea
Slatina
Piatra Olt
BUCHAREST
Balș
Videle
Mihăilești
Jilava
Budești
Roșiori de Vede
Oltenița
Caracal
Olt
Câmpia
Română
Giurgiu
Dunav (Danube)
Alexandria
Piatra
Ruse
BULGARIA
Turnu Măgurele
Zimnicea
Chrni Lom
Razgrad
Pleven

Hungary
Romania
Serbia
Bulgaria
Bucharest
Greece
Turkey

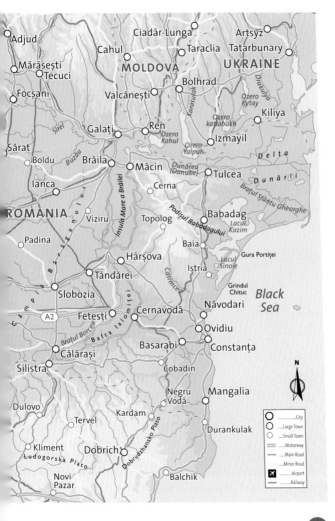

Basarab and his wife remain miraculously intact. The rest of the
monastery complex dates from 1775–8, when it was expanded
by Ghenadie Petrescu, patriarch of the Romanian Orthodox
Church. In the monastery's museum is a fine collection of
religious art, including icons painted by the Romanian maestro
Nicolae Grigorescu.

🅐 Manastirea Caldarușani, Sat Lipia, Comuna Snagov

🔺 *Caldarușani Monastery, southeast of Snagov Lake*

Mănastirea Snagov (Snagov Monastery)

Snagov's main attraction for visitors is the monastery on a
tiny island in the middle of the lake, which reputedly contains
the headless body of Vlad III Țepeș, the inspiration behind the
Dracula myth. The monastery was founded in 1408 by Mircea
cel Batran (Mircea the Old), though rebuilt from 1512 to 1521
during the reign of Neagoe Basarab, and modelled on the

church of Mount Athos in Greece. It is Basarab who, alongside his wife, appears in the votive frescoes inside the church. On the opposite wall are rich paintings of another Wallachian ruler, Mircea Ciobanul (Mircea the Shepherd), and the whole ensemble represents the largest collection of medieval paintings in southern Romania. The tomb of Vlad III Țepeș is found underneath the church, marked only by a painting of Vlad. The church and tower in front of it are all that remains of the original monastery, the other buildings on the island having been added over the following centuries. The only way to get to the island is from the south side of the lake in a self-rowed hired boat from the Complex Turistic Snagov.

ⓐ Sat Siliștea Snagovului, Comuna Snagov

Media Pro Film Studios
Once the state-run film studio that created epics of heroic proportions featuring Romanians doing victorious battle with the Turks, Romans and Hungarians, Buftea was acquired

DRACULA LAND
Romania has long hoped to cash in on the Dracula myth, and for a decade has been toying with the idea of setting up a Dracula theme park. The first attempt was in the Transylvanian town of Sighișoara, but local opposition and embezzlement of funds saw the project get no further than the planning stage. The latest proposals for 'Dracula Land' centre on Snagov Lake, where the local council and population have been far more open to the idea.

🔺 *The splendid setting of Mogoșoaia Palace*

recently by the team behind Pro TV, Romania's leading
television station, and has quickly become world renowned.
A number of major, award-winning movies have been
filmed here, as well as the two-part drama, *Sex Traffic*, the
winner of eight BAFTAs and numerous other awards in 2005.
The studios are vast and the management has recently begun
opening them up to visitors, eager to show what the Romanian
film industry is capable of. What's more, tours are free; you just
need to book a day or two in advance.

ⓐ Str Studioului 1, Buftea ⓣ (031) 825 18 40
ⓦ www.mediaprostudios.ro

Palatul Mogoșoaia (Mogoșoaia Palace)
Some 14 km (8½ miles) north of the capital, Mogoșoaia is today a
growing, middle-class suburb of Bucharest. The great
Renaissance man Constantin Brâncoveanu – prince, politician
and the dominant force in late 17th-century Wallachia – built
himself a palace here in 1680. In 1688 Brâncoveanu, by then
Prince of Wallachia, moved his entire court here, and a village
grew around the palace, including a tiny but wonderful church
which is usually the first thing visitors see. The six short
columns that support the church's portico were much copied by
18th- and 19th-century Romanian architects, giving rise to a
style that became known as Brâncovenesque. Brâncoveanu
and his entire family are superbly depicted on the church's
interior walls.

The main attraction of the complex is of course the palace
itself, a vast and richly decorated building surrounded by well-
kept grounds ideal for picnics. Much of the furniture on display

is original, as is the décor, including more portraits of
Brâncoveanu and his family.

🅐 Valea Parcului 1, Comuna Mogoșoaia 🕻 (021) 312 88 94

🕙 10.00–17.00 Tues–Fri, 10.00–18.00 Sat & Sun, closed Mon

RETAIL THERAPY

There is very little in the way of shops or retail opportunities
around Bucharest, though a huge shopping centre (what will be
the city's largest) is currently under construction at Baneasa
(halfway between Aurel Vlaicu and Otopeni airports), with its
first stores due to open in mid-2008.

TAKING A BREAK

Lions £ Tasty, cheap pizza and pasta at Snagov, which claims to
have the best ice cream in the area; justifiably, so it turns out.
🅐 Sat Snagov, Comuna Snagov 🕻 0724 16 02 12 🕙 10.00–24.00

Casa Romaneasca ££ Large, tasty portions of excellent Romanian
dishes, including the best *mici* (small tangy meatballs, a
speciality of Wallachia) you'll ever taste. Service can be a bit
slow and staff inattentive, however. 🅐 Calea Bucureștilor 258
🕻 (021) 236 15 10 🕙 10.00–24.00

AFTER DARK

Mogoșoaia Palace Restaurant ££ Inside one of the largest and
grandest rooms of the palace this superb restaurant serves

outstanding traditional Romanian food at thoroughly decent prices. ⓐ Valea Parcului 1, Comuna Mogoșoaia ⓣ (021) 312 88 94 ⓛ 12.00–22.00 Tues–Sun, closed Mon ⓘ booked out for weddings almost every weekend in summer

Vânatorul ££ 'The Hunter' unsurprisingly serves game dishes of all kinds in a superb setting on the edge of Snagov Forest. More standard Romanian specialities are also found on the menu, and a live Gypsy band knocks out enjoyable but loud music most summer evenings. ⓐ Sat Snagov, Comuna Snagov ⓛ 11.30–23.00

Al Casolare £££ Never before has the phrase 'just like Mother cooks at home' been more appropriate. Why? Because this restaurant is someone's home and the chef is someone's mother (the waiter's). The food is top-class Italian, served in enormous portions. ⓐ Șos București-Targoviste Km 45, Comuna Mogoșoaia ⓣ (021) 225 41 86 ⓛ 18.00–24.00 Tues–Fri, 12.00–03.00 Sat & Sun, closed Mon ⓘ reservations compulsory

ACCOMMODATION

Complex Astoria Snagov £ On the southern edge of Snagov Lake, there's a choice of 2- or 3-star accommodation in a motel, in small wooden villas, or in bungalows, on-site tennis courts and children's playground included. ⓐ Sat Snagov, Comuna Snagov ⓣ (021) 314 83 20 or (021) 794 04 60

Confort £ Budget choice close to the main airport, Otopeni, with poor location but large rooms and an unexpectedly good on-site restaurant. Most used by provincial Romanians who have to catch early flights. ⓐ Calea Bucureștilor 255 ⓣ (021) 350 41 10 ⓕ (021) 350 41 17 ⓦ www.conforthotels.ro

Motanul Galanton £ Small but classy little *pension* in Ghermanești. Ten rooms, all with great beds and bathrooms, with larger rooms available for families. Small outdoor swimming pool, gym, sauna and great breakfast included. ⓐ Șos Ghermanești 18, Sat Ghermanești ⓣ (021) 491 06 39 ⓦ www.motanulgalanton.ro

Golden Tulip Sky Gate ££ Opposite the entrance to Bucharest's main airport, this hotel is a smart place with a host of luxury extras. A good location if you're planning to explore the surrounding monasteries by car. Transfers to and from terminals and a great breakfast are included in the price. ⓐ Calea Bucureștilor 283 ⓣ (021) 203 65 00 ⓕ (021) 203 65 10 ⓦ www.goldentulipskygate.com ⓔ office@goldentulipskygate.com

Sinaia

Sinaia is a small town 99 km (61½ miles) north of Bucharest, noted for its outstanding hiking in the Bucegi range during summer months, and some wild and challenging skiing during the winter. The town takes its name from its monastery, founded in 1695 by Romanian nobleman Mihai Cantacuzino after a pilgrimage to Mt Sinai in Egypt. The town, situated at an altitude of 800 m (2,625 ft), became a fashionable mountain resort after Carol I built his summer palace here, Peleş, at the end of the 19th century.

GETTING THERE

It takes about two hours to get to Sinaia from the capital, and the best way to do so is by train; fast intercity services from Bucharest to Brasov stop here. Tickets can be bought one hour before departure from Gara de Nord station, or further in advance from the CFR booking office in the city centre (ⓐ Strada Domnita Anastasia 10–14 ❶ (021) 313 26 43 ❷ 07.30–19.30

> ### WHEN TO VISIT
> If you can, avoid visiting Sinaia on winter weekends, when the capital's skiers flock here. If you come during the week you will often have the slopes to yourself. Likewise in summer, avoid weekends in August, when once again the hotels and villas are full of Bucharest residents escaping the summer heat.

Mon–Fri, 08.00–12.00 Sat, closed Sun). Sinaia's railway station is at the bottom of the town, and it's a steep climb up to the main street Bulevardul Carol I. The station is an elegant pile, built to accommodate the Orient Express, which passed through here on its way to Istanbul. Driving here can take a little longer as the road up is narrow and steep in places, with plenty of hairpin bends. If you do choose to drive, follow signs for Ploiești from the north of the capital, and from there Brasov. The main Bucharest–Brasov road runs through the middle of the resort.

◢ *The intercity train to Brasov stops at Sinaia*

⬤ *Head to the Bucegi Mountains for excellent hiking*

SIGHTS & ATTRACTIONS

Hiking in the Bucegi

The mountains which overlook Sinaia, the Bucegi, may not be the highest in Europe but they are certainly among the most spectacular. Jagged stone peaks poke into the clouds and a host of natural wonders dot the landscape, from the Sphinx-like rock over at neighbouring Bușteni to the highland lake Bolboci. The range is criss-crossed with a vast number of hiking trails of all levels. Beginners are best to take the cable car up to the top of the mountain and simply walk down. The plateau at Sinaia Cota 2000, at the top of the cable car, is a great spot for a picnic. Another popular walk for day-trippers is from Sinaia Cota 2000 over to Cabana Ciorcaila and then down to Bușteni via La Scara, a sensational natural stone stairway that passes the equally remarkable Cascada Urlatoarea (Shrieking Waterfall). From Bușteni a taxi or train will take you back to Sinaia. More experienced hikers can use Sinaia as a base to explore much of the mid-Carpathians. There are routes from Sinaia over to Bran, Rașnov and Moieciu de Sus. Cabins dot the mountains and offer food and beds for the night.

Even if you are just setting out for a day trip on one of the well-marked routes, you should always be prepared for bad weather; take warm clothing, water and chocolate. Never set off without a decent map (a good one can be purchased at the cable-car station) and always stick to marked tracks.

ⓐ Cable car: Str Telefericului ⓛ 08.45–15.45 Dec–Feb; 08.30–16.30 Mar–May; 09.00–17.00 June–Oct; closed Nov

The enchanting Peleș Castle in Sinaia is a must-see

Castelul Peleș (Peleș Castle)

Set 100 m (328 ft) or so above Sinaia, this magnificent castle is straight out of a fairytale. The first King of Romania, Carol I, visited Sinaia in 1866 to stay at the monastery and fell in love with the place. He bought land here seven years later and had Wilhelm Doderer, a German architect, build this palace as a summer retreat. Work was not finally completed until 1904. The compulsorily guided tour takes in all of the more exotic rooms of the palace, decorated by artists from all over Europe. Some rooms are replicas of Turkish and Moorish castle halls, others are decorated in more conventional neo-Renaissance style. In the grounds is the smaller but, for many, more tasteful Pelișor (Little Peleș) castle, built for Carol's heir Ferdinand and his English wife Queen Marie. A separate entrance ticket is needed for this. Tickets for both Pelișor and the main palace tour have to be purchased at the entrance gate to the grounds.

ⓐ Str Peleșului 2 ❶ 0244 31 21 84 ❷ 09.15–16.15 Tues & Thur–Sun, 11.00–16.15 Wed, closed Mon. Admission charge

Mănastirea Sinaia (Sinaia Monastery)

The pick of the buildings at the Sinaia Monastery is the tiny, white 1695 monastery church which boasts some of the oldest frescoes in this part of Romania. Recently renovated, the paintings on the portal, depicting the Last Judgement in graphic detail, date back to the church's construction. The gorgeous neoclassical porch that protects the frescoes from the elements was added in the 19th century. Equally striking is the larger and newer of the monastery's churches, the neo-Byzantine red and white building that dominates the centre of the site. Built in 1842

⬤ The neo-Byzantine church at the Sinaia Monastery

it boasts some superb gold-leaf murals and a wonderful carved oak altar. There is also a museum on site containing hundreds of Orthodox religious relics, from illustrated Slavonic Bibles to liturgical robes. In the Paraclis, a small chapel in the corner of the monastery, are more 3,000-year-old frescoes.

🅐 Str Mănăstirii ☎ 0244 31 49 17 🕒 8.30–16.30. Admission charge

Skiing

Sinaia is best known internationally for its skiing, which became far more accessible in 2006 with the opening of a brand new four-man chairlift to whisk skiers up from Cota 1400 to the main ski area, the Valea Dorului. Situated at 2,000 m (6,561 ft) the skiing up here is open and cruisy, and is served by two chairlifts and three drags. Snow is guaranteed right into May. To get to the new chairlift at Cota 1400, skiers still need to take the old cable car from the town (find it behind the New Montana Hotel). This becomes a bottleneck at weekends and queues can be long. To avoid this, stay at the Hotel Cota 1400 (see page 125).

SKIING PRACTICALITIES
Ski hire can be arranged at any of the main hotels, or at a number of ski hire shacks at the cable-car station, where lift passes are also sold. Budget 70 lei for a day's ski hire, and 50 lei for a day's lift pass. Sinaia is not geared to beginners, and arranging ski lessons is a little difficult. The ski schools are all based at Cota 1400, and you need to take the cable car up to find an instructor. Negotiate with the instructors directly; 30 lei per hour is a good price.

When the snow is good there are two challenging routes all the way from the top station down to the resort; there's a drop of over 1,000 m (3,280 ft) and a good 15 km (9 miles) of skiing. If the snow is poor you need to take the cable back down to the resort, so ensure you check the final departure time. Officially the resort has 25 km (15½ miles) of marked pistes; modest by international standards but far more than any other ski area in Romania.
ⓐ Cable car: Str Telefericului ⏱ 08.45–15.45 Dec–Feb; 08.30–16.30 Mar–May; 09.00–17.00 June–Oct; closed Nov

TAKING A BREAK

Brutaria Deutschland £ Still knocking out terrific pastries and average coffee after more than a decade, this place is a firm favourite among regular visitors to Sinaia. Pay for your order in advance at the counter and staff will bring it to you. ⓐ B-dul Carol I 8 ☎ 0244 31 25 52 ⏱ 08.00–22.00 Sun–Thur, 08.00–23.00 Fri, 08.00–24.00 Sat

Cabana Schiorilor £ You can sit on the terrace here summer or winter. Inexpensive, unfussy Romanian cuisine is served by friendly, happy staff. ⓐ Drumul Cotei 7 ☎ 0244 31 36 55 🖷 (021) 0244 31 50 25 ⓦ www.cabanaschiorilor.ro ⓔ schimont@yahoo.com ⏱ 08.00–22.00

AFTER DARK

Beraria Cerbul ££ Just how a beer hall should be, with good cheap beer made on the premises served in huge glasses by

buxom waitresses in Saxon garb. Good food too, if slow to arrive.
ⓐ B-dul Carol I 19 ⓣ 0244 31 47 24 ⓛ 09.00–23.00

Old Nic Pub ££ Decent pizzas are served at cheap prices in an
enormous pub on Sinaia's main street. Service can be terrible
and getting a table without a reservation tough during the ski
season. Lively later in the evening when it doubles as the
resort's main nightspot. ⓐ B-dul Carol 22 ⓣ 0244 31 24 91
ⓦ www.oldnickpub.ro ⓛ 09.00–03.00

Taverna Sarbului £££ The original Taverna Sarbului (there is
a less celebrated sister establishment in Bucharest) is a joy
of meaty treats, including a good selection of game dishes,
served in enormous portions at decent prices. Not a place
for vegetarians. ⓐ Calea Codrului ⓣ 0244 17 12 00
ⓛ 12.00–01.00

ACCOMMODATION

Sinaia £ A basic 3-star package holiday hotel expensively
facelifted. Rooms are small but all have balconies with great
mountain views, bathrooms and oversized televisions. The hotel
has a small indoor, heated swimming pool. ⓐ B-dul Carol I 8
ⓣ 0244 31 15 51 ⓦ www.mmc.ro/sinaia
ⓔ sinaia@mmc.ro

Hotel Cota 1400 ££ If you really like the mountains, or just
simply want to make sure that you are first on the ski slopes
in the morning, where else better to stay than halfway up

the cable car? The hotel was fully renovated in 2006 and boasts large, well-equipped rooms with, naturally, fantastic views. Restaurant and bar too. ⓐ Drumul Cotei ⓣ 0244 31 49 74

Palace ££ Sinaia's once classy Palace hotel, built in 1911, retains a kind of faded grandeur that sets it apart from the modern beats that dominate the centre of the resort. Rooms are huge if spartan, the restaurant a neoclassical gem, and the park surroundings quiet and relaxed. ⓐ Str Octavian Goga 4 ⓣ 0244 31 20 51

International £££ Sinaia's most luxurious hotel is this renovated 1970s high-rise that sits commandingly at the entrance to the resort. Decent-sized – though a tad overpriced – rooms with enormous baths, efficient staff and great views from even the lower floors. ⓐ Str Avram Iancu 1 ⓣ 0244 31 38 51 ⓦ www.international-sinaia.ro ⓔ office@international-sinaia.ro

New Montana £££ Great breakfast and decent 3-star accommodation ideal for the cable car, which is directly behind the hotel. The large swimming pool is open to non-guests (ⓛ 07.00–18.00. Admission charge). ⓐ B-dul Carol I 24 ⓣ 0244 31 27 51 ⓦ www.newmontana.ro ⓔ office@newmontana.ro

---

◉ *Hustle and bustle along the Piața Unirii*

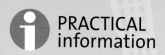

PRACTICAL
information

Directory

GETTING THERE

You are most likely to arrive in Bucharest by air, with direct flights from the UK, Ireland and North America. Arriving by train costs considerably more, and is only really an option if you are visiting Romania on a larger European tour. Driving would take forever and is not really worth considering.

By air from the UK & Ireland

British Airways and Tarom (Romania's national airline) fly direct, twice daily from London Heathrow in around 3 hours and 30 minutes, but their fares are expensive. Wizzair and SkyEurope fly direct from Luton with reasonable fares, though as with all budget airlines the sooner in advance you book the cheaper the ticket is. Another option is to travel via another European city; Alitalia is usually worth checking out, as it often has very good prices on routes to Romanian cities via Milan and Rome. From Ireland, Tarom has direct flights from Dublin.

Alitalia ℹ 0870 544 8259 Ⓦ www.alitalia.co.uk
British Airways ℹ 0845 773 33 77 Ⓦ www.ba.com
SkyEurope Ⓦ www1.skyeurope.com
Tarom ℹ 020 7224 36 96 Ⓦ www.tarom.ro
Wizzair Ⓦ www.wizzair.com

Many people are aware that air travel emits CO_2, which contributes to climate change. You may be interested in the possibility of lessening the environmental impact of your flight

through the charity Climate Care, which offsets your CO_2 by funding environmental projects around the world. Visit
ⓦ www.climatecare.org

By rail from the UK & Ireland
At the time of writing it is not possible to buy a through ticket from London or Dublin to Bucharest. The closest you can get is a ticket to Budapest, from where there is a choice of four daily trains to Bucharest (taking from 12 to 15 hours). It takes around 24 hours to get to Budapest from London.
Rail Europe ⓦ www.raileurope.co.uk
The Man in Seat 61 ⓦ www.seat61.com
Thomas Cook European Rail Timetable ☎ 01733 416477 (UK), 1800 322 3834 (US) ⓦ www.thomascookpublishing.com

TRAVEL INSURANCE
It is important to take out adequate personal travel insurance covering medical expenses, theft, loss, repatriation, personal liability and cancellation. EU citizens with a European Health Insurance Card (EHIC – apply online at ⓦ www.dh.gov.uk/travellers) will enjoy some free or reduced healthcare, but are advised to have private medical insurance as well. If you are travelling in your own vehicle, make sure you have the appropriate insurance, and remember to pack the insurance documents and your driving licence. You will need to make a police report for non-medical claims and ensure you keep any receipts for medical treatment. Consider keeping a copy of your policy and emergency contact numbers in your email account.

ENTRY FORMALITIES
Visas
Citizens from other European Union countries may enter Romania visa-free and stay for as long as they please. Visitors from the US, Australia, New Zealand and Canada can all enter without a visa, but may stay just for 30 days (90 days for Americans). Romanian legislation requires you to have some form of identification on you at all times. A copy of your passport will suffice.

Customs
While Romania imposes no limits on goods imported from or exported to the rest of the EU, your home country may impose its own limits on the amount of cigarettes and alcohol you may bring home.

MONEY
The Romanian currency is the leu (plural lei). It is usually written in full, though sometimes carries the abbreviation RON. One leu is equal to 100 bani. The denominations for notes are 1, 5, 10, 50, 100 and 500; there are coins in denominations of 50, 10, 5 and 1 bani. Many shops and stores (especially electrical shops) will list prices in lei and euros, but note that euros are not legal tender.

It is all but impossible to obtain Romanian currency outside the country, but there is no need to do so as there are ATMs at all of the country's arrival points, and in thousands of locations all over the country. ATMs accept Visa and MasterCard and are the best places to get your hands on lei. Avoid using bureaux de change as they charge exorbitant commissions and offer poor rates of exchange. If you do have to change cash, do it inside a

bank. Traveller's cheques are met with derision everywhere in
Bucharest and are notoriously difficult to get rid of. You will find
it difficult to exchange lei outside of Romania, so try not to
withdraw too much at any one time.

HEALTH, SAFETY & CRIME

Tap water is perfectly safe to drink but given the low price of the
bottled variety, nobody actually does. For any minor disorders any
pharmacy (*farmacie*) will be able to help; you can buy far more
drugs over the counter in Romania than you can at home. Most
pharmacies have English-speaking staff, but few are open 24 hours;
exceptions are HelpNet and Senisblu (see 'Emergencies' page 138). If
you need serious medical attention head for a private medical clinic,
such as one of those listed in 'Emergencies' (page 138).

Bucharest is a remarkably safe city, and there is virtually no
violent crime. Petty crime is a problem, however, so be extra
careful when travelling on buses and trams, where
pickpocketing is rife, and don't flash your wallet around.

The biggest safety issue you are likely to have to deal with in
Bucharest is the city's 70,000-strong stray dog population.
Though mostly harmless, in 2006 one such dog attacked and

DODGY MONEY

Beware of old Romanian notes, which were replaced by the
current ones in 2005; they look the same but are slightly
larger and have four extra zeros. They are no longer legal
tender. If you do get passed one by mistake, you can
change it in a bank.

killed a Japanese businessman. More than 50 people a day are bitten (not fatally) by dogs, but most of the city's population refuse to allow a cull. If you are bitten, get to hospital immediately to have the wound cleaned and get an anti-rabies injection. Though strays are seen more often in the suburbs than in the very heart of the city, you should prepare yourself for at least one encounter with barking dogs. Stay calm, carry on walking and, whatever you do, do not run!

OPENING HOURS

Opening hours of museums are generally 10.00–17.00, and almost all are closed on Mondays. Less well-frequented museums may close early or over lunchtime without warning. Churches are usually open from dawn to dusk. Banking hours are 09.00–17.00 Mon–Thur, 09.00–15.00 Fri, closed Sat & Sun. General shopping hours are 09.30–19.00, though these are extending, often to 21.00. Most shops – except big malls and shopping centres – close at 14.00 on Saturdays, and do not open on Mondays. The small kiosks that litter the city centre to sell cigarettes, drinks and snacks generally stay open 24 hours.

TOILETS

There is no such thing as a decent public toilet in Bucharest. Bearable public toilets (which cost around 0.50 lei to use) can be found in the passage underneath Piaţa Universităţii, in Unirea department store and at Gara de Nord. There are also portaloos in most of the city's parks. Note that if you want to use the ubiquitous McToilet you will need to buy something first; you need the four-digit code on your receipt to enter a McDonald's

toilet. Staff in cafés, pubs and restaurants will get annoyed if
you pop in just to use the toilet; ask first and leave a small tip.

CHILDREN

There are few attractions geared towards children. One big
exception is the **Village Museum** (see page 97), which children
find great fun, as they can climb in and out of the old wooden
houses. The **Grigore Antipa Museum of Natural History**
(see page 95) is also relatively interesting for children. The
Ecvahalis Equestrian Centre (see page 35) opposite the zoo has
pony trekking and riding lessons for kids. There are bowling and
amusement arcades at both the **Bucureşti Mall** and **Plaza
Romania** (see page 35) too. You can also take the kids to Sunday
brunch at one of the big hotels (either Athénée Palace or J W
Marriott); kids usually eat for free and clowns, carers and DVDs
will keep them happy while you enjoy your food and
champagne. The parks all have well-equipped children's play

○ Gara de Nord, the city's main railway station

133

areas, though don't expect health and safety standards to match what you are used to at home.

The following are a few other genuine children's options that may come to the rescue of desperate parents:

Boom Boom Land A smaller version of Children's Island (see below), in the south of the city, with bouncy castles, slides and the like. In summer there are outdoor activities too. ⓐ B-dul Tineretului ⏱ 10.00–21.00. Admission charge

Grădina Zoologică (Zoo) Despite some recent improvements it remains a bit of a sorry place. ⓐ Str Vadul Moldovei 4 ☎ 633 05 02/633 29 51 ⏱ 10.00–17.00 Tues–Sun, closed Mon

Insula Copiilor (Children's Island) A large children's playground with everything from inflatables to adventure trails, set on an island in the middle of Herăstrău Park. You can get to it by taxi or, more fun, by boat with the Herăstrău Lake launches. ⓐ Parcul Herăstrău ⓦ www.insulacopiilor.ro ⏱ 10.00–21.00

Kids' Planet A large indoor playground where children can play while parents enjoy a coffee. It gets very crowded when it rains. ⓐ Piața Alba Iuliu 2 ☎ (021) 326 60 46 ⏱ 11.00–21.00

COMMUNICATIONS
Public telephones
There are few public telephones in Bucharest, and all of them require a Romtelecom phone card. These can be bought from post offices or from most newsstands and kiosks, and cost

10–20 lei. Look out for the sign saying 'Avem cartele Romtelecom' ('We have Romtelecom phonecards').

Mobiles

There are three heavily competing mobile operators in Romania: Vodafone, Orange and Cosmote. All cover the entire city and reception is always good. Bucharest recently went BlackBerry, so you will be able to receive and send emails too. Check with your home network before departure, however, regarding the cost of making and receiving calls and SMS messages, as they are usually very high.

Internet

Most good hotels provide free internet access and there are various WiFi hotspots throughout the city, though they are not usually free beyond the first 10 minutes; you will need an access card from Zapp (ⓦ ww.zapp.ro) or Vodafone (ⓦ www.vodafone.ro). The best internet café in the city is at the British Council (ⓐ Calea Dorobanților 14 ⓣ (021) 307 96 00 ⓦ www.britishcouncil.ro ⓛ 09.30–20.00). PC Net Café (ⓐ Calea Victoriei 120) is smoky but conveniently open 24 hours.

Postal services

The Central Post Office is at Str Matei Millo 1 and stays open 24 hours, 7 days a week. Sending letters and postcards anywhere in the world is relatively cheap, but they can take a long time to arrive.

TELEPHONING ROMANIA
To phone Bucharest from abroad, dial your international access code (usually 00), Romania's country code (40), followed by the Bucharest area code minus the initial 0 (21), and the local seven-digit number.

TELEPHONING WITHIN ROMANIA
For local calls just dial the seven-digit number. If calling Bucharest from elsewhere in Romania (or when calling from a mobile) use the city code (021) too. Mobile phone numbers all have a four-digit prefix beginning with 07.

TELEPHONING ABROAD
Dial the international access code (00), followed by your country code, area code without the initial zero, and the number itself.

Country codes:
Australia 61
Canada 1
France 33
Germany 49
Ireland 353
New Zealand 64
South Africa 27
UK 44
USA 1
Directory enquiries 155

ELECTRICITY

The electricity supply is standard continental European 220 V, 50 Hz, which means that European appliances will work without a problem. Plugs are also standard European, with two round pins. If coming from the UK or US, you will need an adaptor, and US visitors will need a transformer as well.

TRAVELLERS WITH DISABILITIES

Bucharest is not at all ready to receive disabled travellers. Its cracked, uneven pavements are a major hurdle, while public transport is completely inaccessible. Most public places are not yet adapted to handle wheelchairs, though EU legislation means that they should be in the mid-term future. Toilets for the disabled are rare.

FURTHER INFORMATION

There is no tourist information office in Bucharest, and you will find yourself relying on hotel staff for most travel tips. The locally produced city guide *Bucharest In Your Pocket* (Ⓦ www.inyourpocket.com/romania/en) is an indispensable resource. The following websites are also helpful:

Ⓦ www.psst.ro

Ⓦ www.romania.org

Ⓦ www.visitromania.com

BACKGROUND READING

Romania, Lucian Boia

Ceaușescu and the Securitate, Dennis Deletant

Theft of a Nation: Romania Since Communism, Tom Gallagher

Balkan Trilogy, Olivia Manning

Emergencies

EMERGENCY NUMBERS

Police ☏ 112 or 955
Fire ☏ 112 or 981
Ambulance ☏ 112 or 961

MEDICAL SERVICES

The main Accident and Emergency Hospital for Bucharest is
Spitalul de Urgenţe (ⓐ Calea Floreasca 8, next to Dinamo
Stadium ☏ (021) 317 01 21), where some staff speak English.
Emergency treatment is free for EU citizens with a valid
European Health Insurance Card (see 'Travel insurance' page 129)
but you will be expected to pay for any drugs as well as 'tip' the
doctors and nurses. Far more satisfactory (but expensive) are
private medical clinics, such as **Medicover**
(ⓐ Calea Plevnei 96 ☏ (021) 310 44 10 🕐 08.00–20.00 Mon–Fri,
08.00–13.00 Sat, closed Sun) or **Euroclinic** (ⓐ Calea Floreasca 14
☏ (021) 200 68 00), which is open 24 hours.

Dental clinics include **BB Clinic** (ⓐ Calea Dorobanţilor 208
☏ (021) 320 01 51, emergencies 0744 49 91 99) and **Dentamerica**
(ⓐ Str Varsovia 4 ☏ (021) 230 26 08), both open 24 hours.

Pharmacies open 24 hours include **HelpNet** (ⓐ B-dul Unirii 24
☏ (021) 335 74 25) and **Sensiblu** (ⓐ Calea Dorobanţilor 65
☏ (021) 211 11 27; ⓐ Piaţa Amzei 10–22 ☏ (021) 303 85 79; ⓐ B-dul
Bălcescu 7 ☏ (021) 212 49 23; ⓐ Str George Enescu 36–40 ☏ (021)
211 53 34).

POLICE

Should you need to report theft for insurance purposes you will have to do so at the police station in the area in which the theft occurred. To find out where that is, ask at the Police Headquarters:

Inspectoratul General al Poliției ⓐ Șos Ștefan cel Mare 13–15
ⓦ www.politiaromana.ro

EMBASSIES & CONSULATES

Australia ⓐ World Trade Centre, Piața Montreal 1, Entrance F
ⓣ (021) 316 75 58
Canada ⓐ Str Nicolae Lorga 36 ⓣ (021) 307 50 50
Ireland ⓐ Str Vasile Lascăr 42–44 ⓣ (021) 212 21 36
UK ⓐ Str Jules Michelet 24 ⓣ (021) 201 73 00
USA ⓐ Str Tudor Arghezi 7–9 ⓣ (021) 200 33 00

EMERGENCY PHRASES

Fire!	Foc!	*Fohc!*
Help!	Ajutor!	*Ajootor!*
Stop!	Stop!	*Stop!*
Call a doctor!	Chemați doctorul!	*Kematz doctorool!*
Call the police!	Chemați poliția!	*Kematz poleetzya!*
Call an ambulance!	Chemați salvarea!	*Kematz salvareya!*

SPOTA CITY IN SECONDS

This great range of pocket city guides will have you in the know in no time. Lightweight and packed with detail on the most important things from shopping and sights to non-stop nightlife, they knock spots off chunkier, clunkier versions. Titles include:

The publishers would like to thank the following individuals and organisations for supplying the copyright photographs for this book: Craig Turp: all photographs except: allOver photography/ Alamy: page 117; Mediafax Foto: pages 36, 103; Pictures Colour Library: pages 7, 19, 21, 28, 42, 47, 49, 83, 111, 118, 120, 122, 133; Romanian National Tourist Office: page 23; Sorin Toma/Mediafax Foto: page 109; World Pictures: pages 3, 9, 51, 59, 127

Copy editor: Anne McGregor
Proofreader: Ian Faulkner

Send your thoughts to
books@thomascook.com

- Found a great bar, club, shop or must-see sight that we don't feature?

- Like to tip us off about any information that needs updating?

- Want to tell us what you love about this handy little guidebook and more importantly how we can make it even handier?

Then here's your chance to tell all! Send us ideas, discoveries and recommendations today and then look out for your valuable input in the next edition of this title. As an extra 'thank you' from Thomas Cook Publishing, you'll be automatically entered into our exciting prize draw.

Send an email to the above address (stating the book's title) or write to: CitySpots Project Editor, Thomas Cook Publishing, PO Box 227, The Thomas Cook Business Park, Unit 18, Coningsby Road, Peterborough PE3 8SB, UK.